CHOOSE YOU!

DR SHARIE COOMBES

For Floyd and Kayleigh.
I'd choose you every time.

A STUDIO PRESS BOOK

First published in the UK in 2020 by Studio Press,
an imprint of Bonnier Books UK,
The Plaza, 535 King's Road, London SW10 0SZ
Owned by Bonnier Books,
Sveavägen 56, Stockholm, Sweden

www.studiopressbooks.co.uk
www.bonnierbooks.co.uk

1 3 5 7 9 10 8 6 4 2

ISBN 978-1-78741-710-6

MIX
Paper from
responsible sources
FSC® C018072

Written by Dr Sharie Coombes
Edited by Frankie Jones
Illustrated by Nic Farrell
Designed by Nia Williams

A CIP catalogue for this book is available from the British Library
Printed and bound in the United Kingdom

CONTENTS

Welcome to
CHOOSE YOU!

This book comes with a health warning – reading it could seriously improve your happiness and wellbeing! Welcome to your very own course of bibliotherapy – or book therapy.

You know those times when you're feeling happy and relaxed and the hours pass by like minutes? Perhaps it happens when you're hanging out with your favourite people, or chilling by yourself in your room listening to music and watching your favourite videos, or maybe when you're doing **THE THING** that you most enjoy like a game, a hobby, something creative, artistic or sporty. How do you feel about your **SELF** in those moments? My guess is you probably feel content, and you have a clear idea of what pleases you, who you are and what you're about.

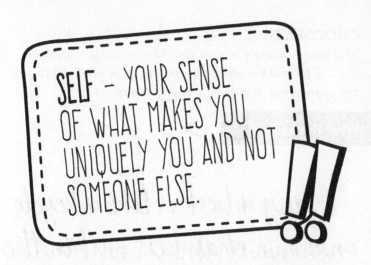

SELF – YOUR SENSE OF WHAT MAKES YOU UNIQUELY YOU AND NOT SOMEONE ELSE.

But there isn't just one version of you, is there? Those other times, when you're feeling awkward, uncomfortable, unhappy or stressed out – how about then? What do you feel or believe about your SELF in those moments? Do you feel in control, confident and capable? If you're like lots of other people and, in particular, lots of other teenagers, you may forget what it is about you that is so great and special at the exact second it would be incredibly helpful to remember. Your sense of who you are might even seem to disappear altogether for a while too. It's a bit like doing a dot-to-dot puzzle with all the numbers missing – and some of the dots too.

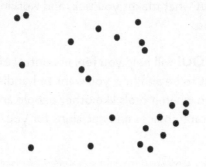

CHOOSE YOU! will help you understand why that happens, discover who you are, choose how you think of your SELF and become more in control of you – all so you can spend your days feeling happy and relaxed.

What this book is*

"Many a book is like a key to unknown chambers within the castle of one's own self."

Franz Kafka

It's not easy being a teenager – everyone else knows what is best for you... well, they think they do, right?

I wrote this book because I want to help you to feel in control of your own life even when it seems that every other person wants to be the boss of you. This book will get you thinking about what makes you tick, and working out how to love being you.

CHOOSE YOU! will help you feel in control of deciding who you want to be and how you want to handle things in your life, even when it feels like other people are making all the important choices and decisions for you. If you're

*Quick answer - It's a book to help you to be happy with who you truly are, now and in the future.

already pretty sure who you are, don't stop reading just yet because there's more! You'll find a load of useful information about your teenage brain and explanations about why it acts the way it does, especially when you feel it's making everything really difficult for you. I'll detail the technical quirks you're up against with a Stone Age brain in the modern world and you'll learn some great hacks to get it working with you when it's going off on one.

I'll introduce you to the carefully devised **CHOOSE YOU! Process** and gently guide you through every step but I'll give you enough space to really make it your own and take from it what you need. The pages are jam-packed with thought-provoking ideas, activities, information, questions, solutions, science, neuroscience, psychology, philosophy and opportunities for self-discovery, self-invention and self-confidence. On top of all that, there's a resources section where I'll provide you with details of organisations you can turn to if you need more support or help at any point in your adolescence.

What this book isn't

This book isn't going to make you feel judged and it's not an instruction manual on how to be a perfect teenager. It isn't a trick to make life easier for the adults around you. It won't lecture you on why you need to be better, cleverer, faster, funnier, richer, tidier or more popular and successful than you already are. And it definitely won't tell you how to be the best, cleverest, funniest, fastest, richest, tidiest or most popular and successful teenager. In fact, it doesn't deal with any sort of competitiveness with your SELF or other people at all*. There's obviously nothing wrong with competitiveness if that's your bag (ask ANYONE who's ever lost a game of UNO™ to me), but that's not the job of this book.

I'll be covering lots of things related to **puberty**** and **adolescence** but **CHOOSE YOU!** isn't your standard book on puberty so it won't give information on everything you might be curious about, like how your body changes and the technicalities of all that. Don't worry though, there's a wealth of excellent books out there in shops and libraries to help you with puberty-specific questions.

Mental health is a very big topic in this book, but this isn't a mental health book that looks in detail at all the different problems humans can experience, nor does it advise you on how to alleviate each of them individually. However, the resources section contains some brilliant websites to help you get any extra information or support you need along the way.

You've also got the internet to search up whatever you fancy and hopefully a **trusted adult** or two to talk to, whether that's at home, at school or in your community. If you find it hard to talk to someone or ask your questions, you'll find the resources section immensely useful. Now that I've covered what this book is and isn't, let's get into why I thought I was the right person to write it for you.

*CORRECTION: This book WILL make you feel happier than you already do (or maybe even feel the happiest you can) – but I reckon that's OK.

See the glossary on page 270 for an explanation of this term and other terms that crop up as we go along: They'll be in **bold italics.

I've spent many years working with teenagers who are going through all kinds of stuff and as a teenager myself (not quite a million years ago), I went through all kinds of stuff that sometimes stopped me from feeling as happy as I'd have liked. I had friends (some of them are still my friends, as you'll see) who went through stuff that was sometimes different to my stuff and I saw how it affected them and got in the way of their happiness too.

I've worked in primary and secondary schools as well as universities and a large London mental health hospital. I kept seeing the same stuff bothering people everywhere I did my job. So, it stands to reason that I decided to study the thing that fascinates me most about humans – **STUFF**. I was especially interested in how feelings and emotions affect us as babies, as we grow up, talk to each other, start school and learn about ourselves and the world. That's why I wrote a really, really, really looong book about it at university and earned a *doctorate** for it.

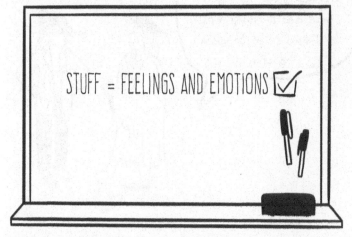

STUFF = FEELINGS AND EMOTIONS ☑

*Remember to check the glossary at the back of the book.

So now I can say:

Trust me, I'm a doctor!

Nope, I don't have a time-machine (not fair!), a sonic screwdriver or a stethoscope. I like to think of myself as a Feelings and Emotions Doctor. Or, a Doctor of Stuff. And someone you can trust.

I dropped my looooong and heavy book on my toe once and it really hurt so I had to go to see a doctor.

A bit later, I trained to be a *psychotherapist* so that I could listen carefully while people talk to me about their stuff. Now, I help them to cope with their stuff and choose what they do with it. Basically, I show them their dots – even some of the invisible ones – then together we join them up, make sense of them and shift the ones that don't seem to fit or that make them unhappy. The picture often changes quite a few times along the way. You'll see exactly how that works as you go through this book.

After I'd been a psychotherapist for quite a while, I was asked to put some of my help and ideas into books for young people to read. So I did. Lots of times.

And then
I met YOU!

> Hi! I'm Dr Sharie and I'm going to be your guide on this journey of discovery, where you'll start joining up your dots and finding, choosing and loving your unique, incredible, happy teenage SELF. You might spot some of the dots I've joined up on the way, too.

Dr Sharie

We've never met, so you might be wondering how I can possibly know what you need. It's true that only you have lived, will live and can live your life and only you will ever know how it feels to be you. It's also true that humans have been figuring out stuff since humans existed. Luckily, lots of these humans have passed down their thoughts over the millennia and because humans have more things in common than they have differences, it's useful to learn from the experiences of others and their reflections on those experiences. That's why I've written some of them down for you over the next 250 pages. Yes, you're unique but you are not alone.

Some of the stuff we go through is not so bad, some feels pretty rubbish and some is just plain confusing. Of course, there's good stuff too, but we can usually handle that already. For the stuff that's not so good, you've now got this book to turn to and there are various ways you could use it.

In addition to taking you through *The CHOOSE YOU! Process*, the chapters contain a variety of activities which will help you to better understand your brain and your life as well as up-to-date information and ideas on how to apply the ideas in your own way. There are fewer activities in some chapters and more in others. You'll find some bits more useful than others depending on your own situation so you can decide what to complete and what to leave out. The activities include spaces for you to record your ideas and thoughts or you could choose to use sticky notes, a notebook or a journal if you prefer.

If you're someone who likes to do things in a set order, you'll be pleased to know that the chapters are designed to provide information in a helpful sequence and move you through **The CHOOSE YOU! Process** smoothly, comfortably and logically. Each chapter focuses on specific aspects of your life but the chapters all relate to each other and will sometimes overlap. At the end of the chapters, you'll find a process grid where you record your thoughts in a numbered box.

If you're someone who's happier to dip in and out and follow your own path, I recommend you start with Chapter One and then read the subsequent chapters in any order depending on what's happening for you at the time and how you're feeling. To make this easier, each chapter starts with a brief description of its key points, so you'll always know what it's about and what to expect. You don't have to use **The CHOOSE YOU! Process** so if you'd prefer to simply do the activities and/or read the information to use in your own way then go ahead! If you are going to use the process but still want to skip between chapters, you can complete the process grids in your own order and review them in order after your final chapter.

Trigger warnings
Look for this logo to alert you that the information you're about to read might be distressing, depending on your individual experiences or worries. Don't be alarmed, there's nothing explicit or graphic in the book at all, I just want you to feel in control and know when something potentially tricky is coming up so you can choose whether to read that part of it.

"You have to believe that the dots will somehow connect in your future."
Steve Jobs

Remember what I said about discovering your SELF? It's like doing a connecting dot-to-dot puzzle that doesn't have all the dots or numbers revealed. Since your birth, you've had to connect the dots that you can see using the information you have available to you at the time. Any dots that you can't see, or that confuse the picture you've made of your SELF so far, can mean you believe wrong or incomplete things about your SELF. Your SELF is continually evolving and will keep doing so – more dots will slowly, or sometimes suddenly, appear and the picture will change again and again. Why not use this book to give yourself a proper say in how that happens? It's time to **CHOOSE** who **YOU** want to be. Whatever experiences you've had to deal with up until now, and whatever tricks your teenage brain likes to play on you, I'll help you join your dots and make sense of them.

Believing incomplete or wrong things about yourself holds you back, stops you from finding your true potential, gets in the way of your happiness and limits how others see you, too. Trust me, you really don't have to be the person that circumstance created – you can build and rebuild your SELF through your whole life if you want.

Any idea what the dot-to-dot picture on the next page might be? As you go through the book, you'll have the chance to try out small sections of this puzzle. By the end, you'll know what and where many of your most important dots are. You'll have cracked this whole puzzle too and you'll be able to see the bigger picture as well as a lot of the finer details. I'll be dropping some enormously hefty clues for you along the way...

Ready to join some of those dots and make a start on giving your SELF the full picture? Great! Let's **CHOOSE YOU!**

turn page on its side

CHAPTER ONE

CHOOSE YOUR SELF!

This chapter will:

1. Help you understand that it's possible to **CHOOSE your SELF!** and know you are not stuck as the person that circumstance created

2. Explain what a **SELF** is and show you how you might already be misunderstanding your **SELF**

3. Break down what truth is and explore different perspectives on truth

4. Help you learn that you can build and rebuild your **SELF**

5. Introduce you to **The CHOOSE YOU! Process**

6. Lead on to Chapter Two

"I am not what happened to me. I am what I choose to become."

Carl Gustav Jung

What is a SELF?

A **SELF** is the idea we have about who we are. Everyone has a SELF. We sometimes call it a sense of SELF, or a SELF concept. Your SELF is different to absolutely everyone else's SELF and that's what makes you unique.

Your SELF is who you believe you are. It's something that exists in your mind because of the way your world has affected or programmed your brain and is what we might call a **construct**. Your SELF changes over time and is not fixed, although you may not always notice it changing.

When you were a baby, you didn't really know which bits of you actually belonged to you and which belonged to whoever was looking after you. Your memory was already forming and your brain and body stored **implicit memories** which helped you to learn automatically from your experiences and get your basic needs met. All this started to shape your SELF. You started to separate or **individuate** from the adults caring for you.

You grew more during the first five years of your life than you ever will again so as you got into toddlerhood, your brain started to develop extremely quickly and your sense of SELF began to emerge.

When your brain could create *explicit memories* (aged around 2 to 3), you would have been able to recall on purpose and repeat things that made you feel good as well as remembering to try to avoid any things that felt bad. These will have changed your sense of SELF. You developed your own likes and dislikes, preferences, wishes and oppositions even if these might have been unpopular with others. You were learning that developing and improving your skills and being in control can feel safe and powerful. This process of *self-determination* happens again in adolescence and can feel really strong and unsettling at times. No one said it would be easy – which is good, because it isn't! But it is possible to make sense of what you experience and **CHOOSE YOU!**

As we saw in the introduction, there isn't just one version of you. Think about when you're laughing with your friends – is that SELF exactly the same as when you're doing something serious with a group of adults? Do you have the same SELF when you're chilling on holiday as you do in an exam? It's possible, but probably not.

Other people will build a version of you in their own minds which will be based on the way the world has affected or programmed their brains. Their individual version of you will be different from yours and from other people's. Sometimes these versions are only a tiny bit different, and sometimes they are massively different. This can be confusing for everyone and annoying for you if you feel like they don't get you or know the real you.

For example, during a conversation with two friends, there are multiple versions of you involved:

- Your own version of you in this specific situation

- Friend A's version of you

- Friend B's version of you

- Friend A's version of what they think is your version of you

- Friend B's version of what they think is your version of you...

Of course, Friend A will also have a version of what they think Friend B's version of you is and vice versa! So, when you are having difficult moments with others, remember they are battling with the version of you they have in their minds based on their own dots, not just your actual SELF. All of which explains why we have fall-outs that we don't always understand or that take us completely by surprise. People are complex! You'll have a head-start on all that human stuff because you're reading this book. You're welcome!

Your SELF constantly evolves throughout your life and you'll usually have a sense of it in three main areas – physical, academic and social. During the teenage years, your views about your body and skills, strengths and weaknesses can all start to put hefty dents in your sense of SELF. Of course happy moments, successes and being acknowledged can also improve it too. Let's make sure that we work towards the goal of improving your sense of SELF.

What's your story?

We are all born at different times, in different places to different adults – OK, I concede that twins, triplets, quadruplets and all the other -lets may have more similarities in these areas than the average human sibling!

Some of us grow up with none, one or both of our biological parents in families with or without other children. Some of us grow up in families that have chosen to raise us and some of us grow up in homes with a variety of unrelated adults and, perhaps, children. Some of us grow up feeling loved and cherished, while some of us don't. Whatever your story, I want you to feel included in the pages of this book because what I have to say affects **YOU**.

Since we all have different circumstances, I'll refer to parents, carers, guardians, other adult family members, teachers, coaches and any other adults in your life as *your adults* throughout the book. After all, books read by adults usually talk about *your children*. As this book is for you, I hope you'll agree that it makes perfect sense to call them your adults!

However you've arrived at this point in your life, you will have had early experiences that have shaped the way you look at the world and the way you see yourself. In subsequent years, you'll have had even more experiences and circumstances to deal with that have exerted a strong influence on your *world view* and attitude to life. These experiences will also have had a lot to do with the way you see other people. If there's been a lot of kindness in your world, you may think everyone will be kind and feel shocked or surprised if someone behaves unkindly towards you. The reverse is also true and kindness from others can feel confusing if you're not used to it.

Who are you?

We'll look at this in a lot more depth in Chapter Two, but it's important to start here.

I've already told you a bit about my SELF in the introduction, but I don't know anything about you, except that you're a teenager who might want to know how to feel happier more of the time. Spend a minute or two thinking about who you are and what's great about you. If you want to, you can write a few lines on the notepad to describe your SELF to me so if we ever meet, we can introduce ourselves.

What would I like about you? What would I admire? Why would I want to spend time in your company? What might we have in common? What might be very different about us? What would your favourite adult say about you?

Pleased to meet you!

WHO AM I?

23

Now, write something negative you believe about yourself.

Now, give yourself a bit more information to work with about this belief:

1. What happened to make you believe this?

2. How long have you believed this?

3. Who else thinks this?

Thank you – we'll use this important information a bit later in the chapter.

What if I could show you that your view of your SELF is incomplete? It's even possible you've been believing all the wrong things about your SELF because you can't see many of your dots, or so far you've only known the version created by other people in their own minds. That version of your SELF may be quite different from your actual SELF.

> OK, from here on I'm going to stop using these large letters and spell self the usual way because I've clearly made my point.
>
> Several times.

The zoology bit!

ALL DOGS ARE AMPHIBIANS
(aren't they?)

Is science your thing? Well, if it is then that's great and you might know all about amphibians already. And if science isn't your thing, it might be after this.

Amphibians are cool (like, literally!) and they come in a variety of different shapes, sizes and colours. They can be found on every continent on the planet, apart from the freezing habitats of Antarctica (I said they're cool, not frozen!). All kinds of creatures are amphibians. Maybe more than you'd realised – before you were today years old.

Perhaps you've seen classification charts like this one before?

ANIMAL CLASSIFICATION
VERTEBRATES

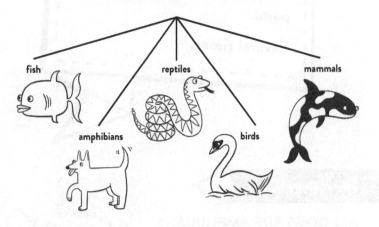

fish

reptiles

mammals

amphibians

birds

Take a closer look. See anything you weren't expecting? It's time for some science! But first a little challenge for you...

Reckon you know your salamanders from your caecilians? Check out the classification chart opposite to test your amphibian knowledge.

VERTEBRATES
AMPHIBIANS

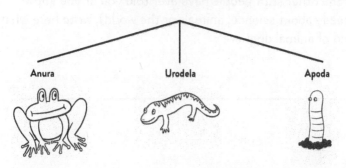

Anura	Urodela	Apoda
Frogs and toads	**Newts and salamanders**	**Caecilians**
Four limbs	Four limbs	No limbs
Webbed feet	Webbed feet	No feet
Can swim	Can swim	Some can swim
Two eyes	Two eyes	Some have eyes
Tail until adult	Tail	

OK, got it? Great, so now take a look at this dog.

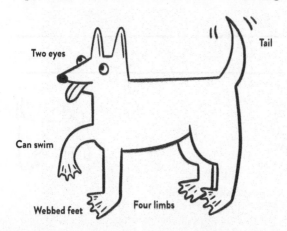

Two eyes

Tail

Can swim

Webbed feet

Four limbs

Using only the evidence from the information on the illustration and classification chart (ignoring absolutely all the other stuff people have ever told you or you know already about science, animals or the world), write here what kind of animal dogs are*:

_____

**

So, according to the evidence, you've **SCIENTIFICALLY PROVED** that all dogs are amphibians, right? **Go you!**

Wait, what? Are you sure? I mean, yes, you've proved it alright from the information in front of you but... aren't you missing something? Let's do a teensy bit of a double-check using more information.

List three **other** characteristics of amphibians:

1. _____

2. _____

3. _____

*HINT – dogs are obviously amphibians, but which type?
**Extra hint – rhymes with sewts and walamanders

List three reasons why dogs might **NOT** be amphibians:

1. _____

2. _____

3. _____

OK, what classification of animals are dogs, actually? This time you can take on board what you already know or looked up, not just the information about dogs I've given you so far.

M_ _ _ _ _ _S

Yep, you're right of course. Take a bow!

Dogs are NOT amphibians.
But just using the limited information on these pages, it was looking that way for a while.

Why does any of this matter?
What this shows is that even having **FIVE points of reference** or bits of evidence from the scientific classification chart wasn't enough to give you the full picture about dogs and amphibians. You were able to prove something to yourself that simply isn't true. Sometimes, the evidence we gather up about ourselves isn't solid enough to define who we really are. We usually make decisions about our strengths or difficulties and what is good or bad about us based on fewer bits of evidence than the five points of reference which **proved** all dogs are amphibians* and, of

*They're not, by the way – and nor are you! But you knew that already.

course, some of that evidence will be other people's opinions not actual proper facts.

In fact, we often make decisions about ourselves based on only three points of reference.

I wonder how often you've made the same mistake about yourself? Times when you've listened to bits of evidence perhaps from yourself or someone else and proved something about **you** that just isn't how things really are.

 A feeling is NOT a fact.

Just because you feel, think or believe something, it doesn't make it a fact. You can believe that all dogs are amphibians (sorry about that!) but believing it doesn't make it true. Let's go back to your negative belief about yourself on page 24. Go back if you need to remind yourself.

Done? OK, look at the questions to get a deeper insight into whether it's actually a fact. It might be true – not all negative beliefs about ourselves are false but you deserve to be sure if you're going to be so critical of yourself. You can write your response if you'd like, or discuss it with someone you feel comfortable with or just think about it by yourself.

Is it true?

_____

What's the evidence for your decision?

_____

What else could it mean?

_____

If you're stuck on this last question, examples here might be 'On that day, I wasn't able to...' or 'Sometimes, I...' or 'I'm still learning to...'

Maybe you've proved more false things in other situations too – in friendships, at school or with your family? Have a look at these examples. Do they ring a bell with you?

You couldn't go to a friend's birthday. You felt you're **obviously** a boring person and they must now hate you.
➤ NOT TRUE!

You messed up a test. You decided you're **obviously** stupid.
➤ NOT TRUE!

A friend or family member was in a bad mood. You thought they **obviously** didn't like you anymore. ➤ NOT TRUE!

Add a few of your own if they spring to mind.

_____

_____

_____

_____

_____

Pick one of these situations and think about it again, using the questions:

Is it true?

_____

What's the evidence for your decision?

_____

What else could it mean?

_____

_____

We'll explore how you can use these questions again later in the book but that'll do for now.

The idea behind 'A FEELING IS NOT A FACT' is complicated. It requires you to grasp the *concept* of there being more than one 'truth' in the whole picture. Understanding this can also be a wonderful relief and allow you to see things differently or at least accept that there may be another explanation for what you feel.

Stories are great for helping us understand complex ideas. Here's a modern retelling of an old folk tale (or parable) which demonstrates the importance of having the whole picture to avoid proving false things to yourself. Sometimes, getting the whole picture or finding the 'truth' isn't straightforward and might mean you need to see things through someone else's eyes. Or hands.

In a hot, dry land lived six blind scholars, who knew each other as well as any sisters and brothers do. They met every afternoon to talk about the world and all the fascinating things in it. For as long as anyone could remember, they had gathered together this way. They were wise and learned folk.

Under the tamarind tree they sat, cross-legged, shading themselves from the fiery sun. They couldn't see its light, but they felt the warmth on their skin and the thirst in their throats.

This day, a villager passed by and told them of a new creature never before seen in that land. They were intrigued and wanted to know everything they could about the animal. The villager promised to bring it at once to the tamarind tree.

And so he did.

The scholars spread themselves out into a circle and stood waiting for the mysterious beast to be brought to them. The villager led the elephant, for that was its name, into the centre of the group. He took them, one by one, towards the elephant until they each could touch it.

The first gasped as she grasped at its side, astounded by the elephant's size. She announced to the others, being the first to touch it, that it was a huge beast which resembled a wall – thick and wide and tall.

The next, a man of quite a height, stood upright and brushed the elephant's ear. For all who might care, he argued, the beast is a creature of flight, with fan-like wings to move the air.

The third scholar to speak took hold of the trunk and declared it to be a lively snake, as might make a mammal quake, dry and hungry enough to snare its living chunk of food.

The next leaned against a leg and its knee, 'Oh, it's a living, moving tree', said she.

The fifth found the tail and wrapped his hands around it with hope. He stated to all that the beast was no bigger than a rope.

The last crept forward in fear, confused by each wildly different idea. He found a tusk, hard, round and sharp, and knew at once he held a spear.

With each new declaration, the scholars grew angrier and each protested the truth of what they could feel with their own fingers. Harsh words were spoken and threats were made in frustration. Years of friendship and learning were at risk of being broken.

The villager took the elephant away, afraid it would come to harm. He told the scholars that each was right, and each was wrong but they should talk to one another to understand how that could be. They must choose to work together and let go of their false certainties to reveal the whole truth, using all six pieces of truth they had to hand.

And so they did.

"Your time is limited, so don't waste it living someone else's life. Don't be trapped by dogma - which is living with the results of other people's thinking. Don't let the noise of others' opinions drown out your own inner voice. And most important, have the courage to follow your heart and intuition."

Steve Jobs

By making important choices about how you see yourself, you'll feel happier, more informed and more in control of your life. That said, you might be wondering, 'What about the things I can't choose?' Well yes, it's true – there are many things in your life you can't choose. These might include:

- Having responsibilities and being accountable to others (family, adults, school, society)

- The past (when or where you were born, mistakes you've made)

- Your genes (but look up *epigenetics* in the glossary and see Chapter Four for more on this)

- The environment and culture your adults and community members grew up in, and the experiences they had which shaped their expectations and sense of SELF

- What other communities and people think, feel, believe or do (but you can influence these which we've seen with Greta Thunberg's campaigning work)

- Getting older

- The weather

But that doesn't mean you can't **CHOOSE** who **YOU** are in the face of these things. You can choose your:

ATTITUDE   BELIEFS   ACTIONS   BEHAVIOUR   RESPONSES

The next few chapters will guide you safely through all this, so that you can take any problem or worry that comes your way and learn to control the thoughts you have about it instead of allowing those thoughts to take control of you, making you feel you have no power to **CHOOSE**. You'll find out how to use your power as you begin working through **The CHOOSE YOU! Process**.

 0000000000000000000000

 Start with the positives!

Write down 3-5 things you like about the person you are already. Examples might be:

- I'm kind to my friends

- I have a good sense of humour

- _____

- _____

- _____

- _____

- _____

Add something that seems to get in the way of your happiness more often than you'd like. For example:

- I sometimes get sad/angry/scared without knowing why

- _____

- _____

- _____

 oooooooooooooooo oo ooo oooo

Let's find out more about how you're going to **CHOOSE YOU!**

The CHOOSE YOU! Process

The process is based on tried and tested techniques used in different forms to help adults and adolescents all over the world. I've refined these effective ideas and created a definitive, structured process specifically for this book to make it really supportive for YOU! It's simple and easy to use and consists of identifying particular things you'd like to focus on to help you feel happier. You'll add brief details to boxes provided at the end of each chapter and practise using the six **CHOOSE YOU!** steps to achieve your goals – you'll find spare grids at the back of the book if you need them. I'll provide examples to give you ideas and help you understand how to use the system but feel free to use it in the way that is the most helpful to you.

Here are the six **CHOOSE YOU!** steps:

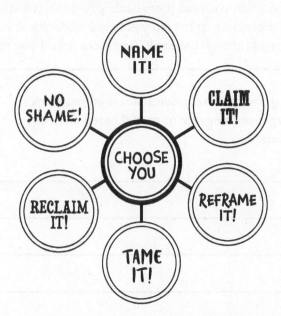

Don't worry if it all seems a bit confusing at the moment – it will make sense once you get started in the next chapter. You'll quickly get used to the steps in **The CHOOSE YOU! Process** and, in doing so, master a skill that can offer you a lifelong ability to manage stress, change and uncertainty, keeping you as healthy and happy as possible.

Go dotty!

We've seen what happens – to dogs and to you – when you make decisions without enough information or evidence. Basically, you take a few points and make a dot-to-dot picture of yourself, the situation, the world and other people, and will often miss out key details that make the picture accurate and complete. Maybe you've uncovered one to two of your own dots in this chapter. If so, write them here and when you read them back, your brain will start joining these dots up to help you better understand yourself as you read through the book. Add more dots if you need to.

- E.g. I'm quite sensitive and sometimes think negative things about myself based on dodgy evidence.

- _____

- _____

- _____

Get connected!

Join up these dots – can you work out what the drawing is going to be, yet? Are there enough numbers or dots to help you make sense of it? You may not be able to tell which side is up!

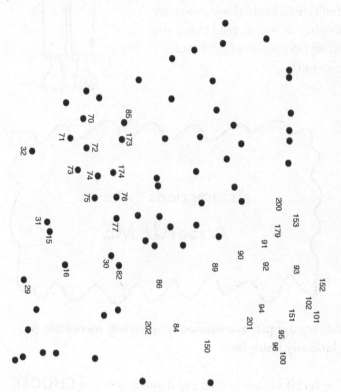

turn page on its side

Working through **CHOOSE YOU!** is going to make sure you don't fall for the same trick about yourself as you (nearly) did about frogs and dogs. It's obviously important that you don't mistakenly think you're an amphibian – or indeed make any other false assumption about yourself!

Assumptions make an

ASSofU&ME

You are **unique, extraordinary, amazing, incredible** and **gloriously imperfect**.

I've said it before and I'll say it again, you can **CHOOSE** who and what **YOU** want to be. It might be too soon for you to decide what specifically you're going to **CHOOSE** to work on just yet so why not read Chapter Two to get to **KNOW your SELF!** better, so you can **NAME IT!** and start **The CHOOSE YOU! Process**...

CHAPTER TWO

NAME IT!

KNOW YOUR SELF!

This chapter will:

1. Focus on the **NAME IT!** section of **The CHOOSE YOU! Process**

2. Break down how to ask questions to challenge yourself and others using critical thinking

3. Help you discover more about who you are so you can **KNOW your SELF!**, find your dots and identify which aspects of yourself you'd like more power to **CHOOSE**

4. Get you understanding what **YOU** think, feel, believe and do as a unique human being (we'll take this further by looking specifically at identity including sexuality and gender in Chapter Seven)

5. Explain the neuroscience of how your brain, body and biological programming work and how these may help and hinder you, me and everyone else

6. Lead on to Chapter Three

"To know yourself is the beginning of all wisdom."

Socrates

Socrates was born in ancient Greece in 470 BC. He was a *philosopher* who spent decades thinking and talking about being a thinking and talking being.

He died in 399 BC.

Philosophers question, challenge and imagine, relentlessly testing ideas on the nature of knowledge, reality and life.

The history bit!

Let's go way back in history to see how all this self stuff started and get a sense of why it's **SO** important. That time-machine would be very useful right now. Alas, we don't have one, so I've done the leg work already to bring you up to date on the back story.

Inscribed at the entrance of the Temple of Delphi in ancient Greece (1200 BC–600 AD) was the saying, 'Know Thyself'. Socrates was inspired by this *maxim* and spent many decades of his own life trying to understand how to do just that. Like Plato (his student) and Aristotle (Plato's student), he spent a lot of his time contemplating and discussing the various ideas he was forming. He started a period of about 150 years of thinking, talking and teaching and is known as the father of western *philosophy*.

Socrates was concerned with what it means to be alive or, as I like to say, with being a being. He went into great depth by examining the nature of living a life and all its many complications. He believed that examining your own self and trying to understand who you are is what truly makes life worth living.

Because he didn't write any of his ideas down, they were passed on through word of mouth and discussions with his students. Those students continued these conversations with their own students. Thankfully, Plato and others wrote down many of the ideas for us to read which lots of people still do to this day.

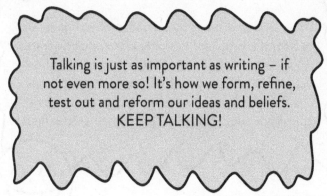

Talking is just as important as writing – if not even more so! It's how we form, refine, test out and reform our ideas and beliefs.
KEEP TALKING!

Socrates devised a way of exploring our thinking which has come to be known as the *Socratic Method*. He asked questions to get to the heart of a thought, feeling, idea or belief using logic and facts wherever possible. Think back to Chapter One when you wrote down something negative about yourself. Remember the three questions I asked you:

- Is it true?

- What's the evidence for your decision?

- What else could it mean?

These Socratic questions are based on the Socratic Method. They help to get to the truth and dig out the facts of the matter. Using them to challenge your thoughts, feelings, ideas or beliefs means you are developing critical thinking. If you get into the habit of using these questions, you'll create a thinking gap that allows you to recognise when you are reacting emotionally to non-facts. You can then give more thought to how you want to react and CHOOSE what you believe about yourself.

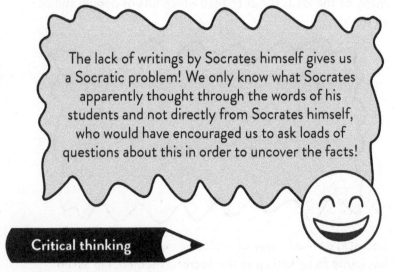

The lack of writings by Socrates himself gives us a Socratic problem! We only know what Socrates apparently thought through the words of his students and not directly from Socrates himself, who would have encouraged us to ask loads of questions about this in order to uncover the facts!

Critical thinking

Critical thinking IS NOT what happens in your head when someone is being super annoying, and you decide they are a bit of a wally. It's not about finding fault with yourself or others.

Critical thinking IS a technique you can learn and, like Socrates, use to dig deeper. It's a way of looking for flaws in thoughts and words that encourages you to question everything and not accept things just as they are presented to you – whether that's by your own mind or by someone else. You can use critical thinking to get to the facts of things you see or read on social media too, including enhanced or edited photographs, videos and images and persuasive political promotion dressed up as 'information'.

Look for an informative or political post on social media.

How do you feel about what you've just read or watched?

Does it match with your beliefs or is it presented from a different perspective?

Look at it or watch it again and try to apply critical thinking to it. Some questions you could ask are:

What are the facts?

_____

Who provided the facts?

_____

Who has paid for those facts to be provided?

_____

Where is the proof for the facts?

_____

What different facts contradict these ones?

_____

How are the facts being used – are they used in the same context for which they were intended?

_____

Have false assumptions been made with those facts?

_____

Are all dogs amphibians?

_____

FAKE NEWS!
I'm choosing a new scarf and tell the shop assistant I don't like the orange one – someone overhears me and tells a friend that Dr Sharie hates oranges and now has a Vitamin C deficiency. And scurvy. And no teeth.

What is truth?

Crikey – that's a tough one! Take a look in the dictionary and see if it says what you were expecting. Does it really make it clear? Philosophers, scientists and all sorts of others have been debating this one since before Socrates was born (when was that, do you recall?). What do you think truth is?

_____

_____

_____

Most people would agree truth is important but, as we've seen, we can't always agree on what the truth is. You see it from your own perspective, which is influenced by your experience. The best I can do is to tell you that truth is an interpretation of something that is generally recognised as reflecting the facts, reality and available evidence, such as, all orange scarves are hideous. Oh wait, no – that's just my own bias!

WHO AM I?

Plenty of philosophers have followed the example of Socrates by thinking about their own thinking* and pondered the 'Who am I?' question – and a multitude of other questions. You'll hear from a few of them as you read on. Now it's your turn to be the philosopher and work out the answers for yourself and about yourself.

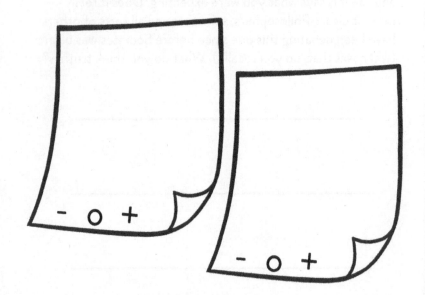

*Thinking about your own thinking is called **metacognition**.

Describe yourself using the first words that come to mind. Fill in these sticky notes with those words or phrases. **Do this without reading any of the further instructions.**

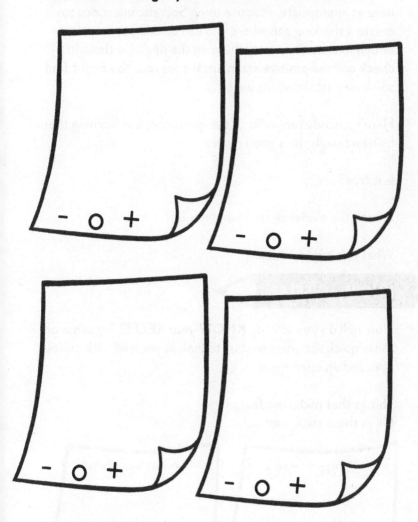

Tip If you're stuck for ideas, focus on whatever's most important to you about yourself – personality, preferences, skills, appearance or anything!

Look at what you've written on the sticky notes. Check which words are positive (+), negative (-) or neither positive or negative (neutral O) and mark the symbols on each sticky note as appropriate. Practise using Socratic questions to create a thinking gap where you can decide between fact or opinion. Don't just try them on the negative thoughts – check out the positive and neutral ones too. You might find some new truths about you!

Here's a handy reminder of the questions, but learning them by heart might be a good move:

Is it true?

What's the evidence for your decision?

What else could it mean?

KNOW your SELF!

How well do you already **KNOW your SELF!**? Try some of these quick activities to start to look at yourself with curious eyes and an open mind.

Things that make me feel...
Fill in these sticky notes.

I'm happiest when...

I'm most excited when...

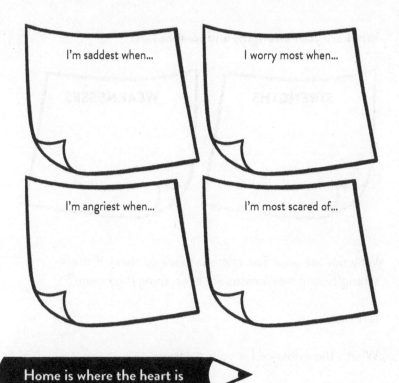

I'm saddest when...

I worry most when...

I'm angriest when...

I'm most scared of...

Home is where the heart is

List all the places where you feel like you're 'at home' – and all the people or things that make you feel 'at home' too. Is there anything in common between these places?

- _____
- _____
- _____
- _____
- _____

What are your strengths and weaknesses?

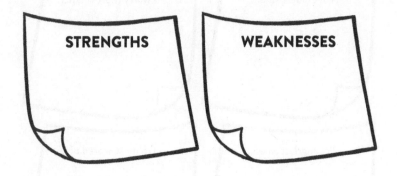

Why not use your Socratic questions to check if these strengths and weaknesses are everything they seem?

Is it true?

What's the evidence for your decision?

What else could it mean?

Me, you and everyone else too

Now you've had the opportunity to begin to develop your thinking gap skills, it seems like a good time to explore what's going on behind the scenes for all of us. There are some quite complex ideas in this section so use the glossary if it's helpful. The following chapters will add more explanation, so you don't have to understand it all here. Your unique, incredible *brain* will join up the dots as you read more.

Brain, body and biology
Thanks to your brain, you can speak, plan, learn, adapt, remember, work stuff out, organise yourself, solve problems,

find things funny and understand complicated information. Your brain sends millions of messages throughout your body every day and night – even when you're asleep.

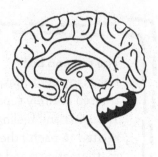

All in your mind

Your brain is responsible for every emotion, sensation, thought and feeling you have. These all start in your brain and they happen whether you want them to or not.

Wait up! Brain or mind?

Well, people use both words for the same thing but there is a technical difference, if you want to be picky...

Your **brain** is the matter or structure made up of brain cells that lives in your skull. It's the most complex organ in your body. Every part of you is linked to and controlled by your brain.

Have you got a few hours to discuss the **mind**? Philosophers and scientists are still arguing over this one and asking ever deeper questions about it. A possible answer is that your *mind* isn't a physical structure or part of your body but is the part of you that is aware of yourself and is the product of your brain and body functions. It can be seen as a construct.

"I think therefore I am."

René Descartes

The religion bit!
For many centuries, the body and mind were
treated entirely separately from one another.
Thoughts and feelings weren't considered
related to each other. Descartes (1596-1650), a
mathematician and philosopher amongst other
things, felt this was the best way so that medicine
could be used for treating a sick body while the
mind could belong to God and not be interfered
with by mere humans.

The neuroscience bit!

Over the last 50 years, there's been a huge amount of
scientific research and we know that the body and brain are
so related that the health of each depends on the other. You
are basically a *brain-body*. You think and feel – sometimes
you'll even do both at the same time! Looking after your
brain and body is important to your happiness and wellbeing
as well as to your mental and physical health. As a teenager,
your brain-body will feel things a lot more than it used to
because it's much more sensitive during adolescence and
responds more intensely to your experiences especially
when other people are part of those experiences. It works
and reacts to the world differently from how it did when you
were younger. It will continue to change even when you're
an adult.

Your brain might have developed like the majority of brains
(*neurotypical*) or like a minority (*neurodiverse* or *neuro*

A-typical), as seen in autism (ASD), dyspraxia (DCD), dyscalculia, dyslexia, dysgraphia, Tourette's Syndrome, ADHD or acquired injury (see Chapter Seven for more explanation of how these affect us). Both brain types have considerable advantages and some difficulties. Just like your fingerprints, your brain is a one-off and is individual to you.

Whether it's neurotypical or neurodiverse, your brain is incredible. Think of both types as games consoles – one's a PS4 and one's an X-BOX. Both are brilliant, fully functional, have great games and different advantages and disadvantages but try putting a PS4 game into an X-BOX, or vice-versa, and there's going to be some technical issues. Use this book to work out your brain type and how to look after it.

Viva Las Vagus!
Ever noticed sensations in your chest and stomach when you have strong feelings? Why is that? Well, your heart and stomach both have their own cluster of brain cells which are always communicating via your vagus nerve with your main brain. I'll tell you more about this incredible superhighway running through your body in Chapter Five.

Here are some more words that are often used to mean the same thing. Again, there are some technical differences for the picky amongst us (OK, mainly me really!) which are explained here to help you understand yourself more. People will understand what you mean whether you use the word emotion or feeling so don't get too caught up on the differences.

Emotion

Emotions happen in the brain in response to a thought, your senses (what you hear, see, touch, smell or taste) or to your inner senses (like tired or hungry, cold or off-balance). An emotion is literally the movement that your brain creates by sending electrical signals zooming around your *central nervous system (CNS)*, which is essentially a racetrack with pit stops in every part of your body (ESPECIALLY in your armpits!). Bursts of chemicals (*hormones* and *neurotransmitters*) pump throughout your body in seconds to fuel the motion of the emotion – somewhat like locomotion (OK, I've stopped now!). You won't always be aware of what has caused the emotion and you cannot directly control it. This is all much more intense in adolescence and can be hard to deal with. In time, you can retrain some of your emotional responses to be more helpful to you, something that's discussed further in Chapter Five.

Neurodiverse brains often experience the information coming from the senses **even more** intensely which can feel very powerful and overwhelming. This is referred to as a *sensory processing* difficulty. I'll cover this more in Chapter Seven.

Feeling

A feeling is your inner experience of the sensations in your mind or body because of an emotion. Happiness, sadness, anger and worry are some feelings you may recognise. You can feel an emotion in any part of your body as well as in your mind. You can't directly control feelings caused by emotions but you can control how you manage them and choose to interpret and respond to them with the right guidance*. Over time, this will give you more control over the feelings you experience.

Thought

A thought is an idea that forms in your mind as a result of the act of thinking. Thoughts can happen on purpose or in response to information, your senses or sensations, and a feeling or emotion. They can also happen spontaneously. Thoughts occur in a range of forms including words, sounds or pictures and might be to do with the past, the present or the future. Thinking is a mental process that lets you create models of understanding, explore your experience of the world and yourself, make decisions, solve problems, develop theories and analyse information.

You can learn to influence your thoughts so that they work for you and so you're not surprised by them or how you react to them. Chapter Five will show you how.

Here's a simplified explanation of how your brain looks and the way it works:

*This book is the right guidance, in case you were wondering!

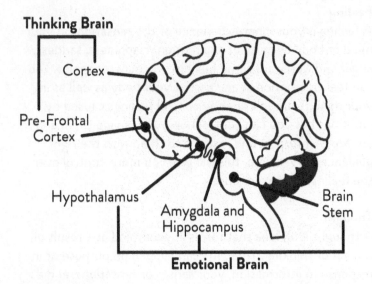

Thinking Brain

Cortex

Pre-Frontal
Cortex

Hypothalamus

Amygdala and
Hippocampus

Brain
Stem

Emotional Brain

Brain stem

This ancient area of your brain controls your vital functions like heart rate, breathing, body temperature and balance. We share this part with all animals, even reptiles (and amphibians!). This part of your brain is stuck in the Stone Age. You have no conscious control over its actions.

Limbic system

Mammals developed this brain region a long time ago. It works closely with the other two areas and is responsible for emotional learning and keeping you safe. Important parts of the limbic system are the *amygdala* (which I call Bob! who you'll meet formally in Chapter Five), the *hypothalamus* and the *hippocampus*. In truth, you have two Bobs, or amygdala – one at either end of your limbic system – but they work together as

one unit. Through some Stone Age programming and a virtual switch mechanism, they quickly team up with the **brain stem** if they sense danger causing you to freeze and experience fight or flight, making you avoid things you find uncomfortable. They're responsible for all your feelings of anxiety, fear and panic, but remember they're doing their absolute best to keep you safe at all times. Your amygdala is a survival mechanism that you need to keep you aware of dangers in your environment. They can team up with the pre-frontal cortex through the switch mechanism but need to be trained by you to do this.

Bob is depicted in this book as a dog – you'll see why later. In your actual brain, Bob consists of two almond shape structures who reside in either side of your brain. Give them faces to remember so when you think about your emotional brain, you can picture Bob.

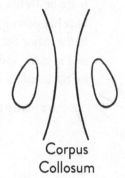

Corpus
Collosum

Pre-frontal cortex

This forms part of the larger cortex which is your **thinking brain** and makes you who you are. It develops after you are born and needs contact with other people for it to flourish. The cortex learns, develops language, thinks and enables you to be creative. The pre-frontal cortex is at the front of your brain above your eyes. It's important for emotional decision making and judgment. It can be taught to take control and help you react differently to emotions and feelings.

Having a brain with an essential part stuck in the Stone Age while you're living in a much safer modern world is interesting to say the least! Ask the oldest adult you know to tell you about the phone they had at your age. If they've still got it, all the better, otherwise search for a picture of it online! Imagine trying to post to Insta or TikTok on that! Not happening! Once it's had a major technical overhaul and system update, it will be up to date and you'll be back online in no time. Same with your brain...

ERROR!

System Update Installing!

In the first five years of your life, your brain developed massively. As you move into the teen years your brain develops almost as massively as it did then, and changes more than it ever will again in your life. Basically, it gets a **dramatic system update** starting a unique phase of development where it reorganises itself. Anything that's out of date, unused or no longer needed gets dismantled, deleted and overwritten. This is called *pruning*. Pruning starts with your emotional brain at the back and works forward to the thinking brain. This can cause a few disruptions for you as you'll feel more emotional, be less logical and find it harder to make good judgments for a while – you may need to ask your adults to remember how this felt when they were teens and maybe even ask them for their help sometimes (**they'll like that – try it!**). You have zero control over when this update takes place – it's automatically downloaded and installed in response to puberty hormones. It can sometimes feel like this happens overnight! Generally, this starts to happen once you begin puberty, and it can peak around the age of fourteen. This does vary from person to person so it's hard to be precise. You will notice it when it happens to you, though.

Building connections

You were born with around 86 billion *neurons* (electrical brain cells) in your brain and about the same number of glial cells (smaller, non-electrical brain cells). Your brain will contain more than 100 trillion connections. Neurons are the brain's building blocks which connect and reconnect with each other throughout your life – a bit like brain LEGO®. However old you live to be, you'll still be growing brain cells and building new connections right up until the end of your life. When pruning happens during your system update, these blocks are pulled apart and reconfigured – this is called *rewiring*. You will lose some of your grey brain matter to make space for more white matter and get a white covering from the glial cells that's like superglue (*myelin*) over your neurons, which will speed up your brain-body electrical signals to be about a hundred times faster than before. Information zooming through your brain will no longer be using the slow, country lanes to get around but will start using the superhighways and motorways. You've got yourself a brain-Ferrari now!

Imagine having a vast set of little LEGO® models you made as a toddler and in primary school using all your best pieces. Since then, those models have been shoved to the back of a cupboard and forgotten about. To make the larger, complicated models that you're now capable of, you're going to have to rummage around in the cupboard and take those old, unused models apart, starting with the ones that were furthest back. Your adolescent brain keeps making bigger and better models by connecting the blocks in different ways. Each new connection is the result of brain cells being moved and pushed together, or *firing and wiring*, while you're learning from experience and studying. Once you've made your new models, the blocks are superglued together. You'll then be able to add or change sections and make more models as you go through life, but this job has to be done first – and it has to be done now. It's hard work. No wonder you feel more sensitive to everything while it's happening!

"Neurons that fire together, wire together."

Donald Hebb

When you learn something and understand it, we call it 'making a connection' because it's when your brain literally makes a connection! When Einstein's brain was examined after his death, it was no bigger or heavier than the average adult brain. However, he had around 15% more connections than the average in the area of the brain responsible for mathematical thinking. It looks like he'd grown his neural networks and improved his brain power.

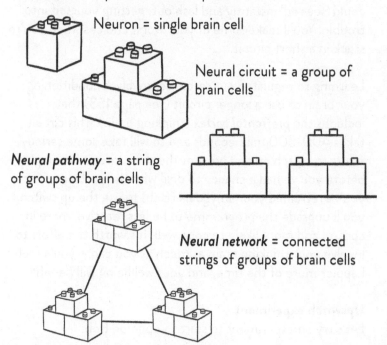

Neuron = single brain cell

Neural circuit = a group of brain cells

Neural pathway = a string of groups of brain cells

Neural network = connected strings of groups of brain cells

Short circuits!

Your *sympathetic nervous system (SNS)* is what causes you to respond to threats and problems with a rush of the hormones *adrenaline* and *cortisol* (see page 153). When you rely on instinctive responses such as anger or anxiety,

your brain uses a short circuit that takes 14 milliseconds to fire off. In a tense situation, it will know there's a problem well before you've had the conscious thought. Your amygdala (Bob) will have pressed the down switch and sent the information to the brain stem so you'll be acting on your instinctive response before you know it. If this is a scary situation, you might freeze, feel

aggressive or run away. If it's one that makes you angry, you could 'see red' instantly and lash out, getting yourself into trouble. You'll make some of your worst choices when you're stuck in a short circuit.

Learning to regulate your responses involves conditioning your brain to use a longer circuit (see page 153) that includes the *prefrontal cortex* (thinking brain). This circuit takes 400-500 milliseconds and so will take some serious effort to switch on and prevent the short circuit blowing up before you've had a chance to deal with the problem. Once you've retrained your amygdala (Bob) to use the up switch, you'll upgrade the programme to be less reactive, more in control and more likely to cope well. It's worth the effort to involve your thinking brain as much as you can – you'll feel happier more of the time, and your wellbeing will benefit.

Upswitch experiment

Let's try an experiment to start to upgrade Bob.

Think of something that makes you a bit nervous or annoyed. Not anything that terrifies or infuriates you, yet! Scale out of 5 how much it bothers you, where one is completely fine and five is the most nervous or angry you could ever imagine being. Describe the situation to someone or write it down. Now, picture yourself doing something you love and notice how you feel on the inside when you do that thing. Keep hold of that feeling while you describe the nervous-making situation again or read back what you've written.

When you can scale the nervous or annoyed feelings as a 1, you'll know you've retrained Bob with that particular situation. That's a brilliant start.

You can use this experiment with as many problems as you like to help Bob upgrade.

Emotional regulation

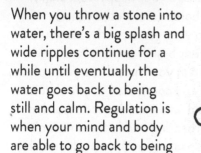

When you throw a stone into water, there's a big splash and wide ripples continue for a while until eventually the water goes back to being still and calm. Regulation is when your mind and body are able to go back to being still and calm after a problem. Your *parasympathetic nervous system (PNS)* is responsible for regulation, also known as rest and digest. There are ways you can help it to work for you, which are discussed further in Chapter Five.

List the ways you've previously used to calm yourself down. Arrange these in order from the most successful to the least. Come back to this list whenever you need a reminder of what works for you.

- _____
- _____
- _____
- _____
- _____
- _____

Memories are made of this

How easily you're able to manage your happy, sad, angry, anxious, excited, frustrated, bored (and all the other) feelings will depend partly on your genes, partly on your environment and partly on your brain's implicit memories from the experiences you had in your first three years of life. If you felt securely attached and connected to your adults as a very young baby and child, and experienced care that was in tune with your needs (bearing in mind you weren't able express these needs by speaking yet), you will probably have felt comforted and calmed by cuddles and loving interactions. This successful early *co-regulation* will have trained your brain to settle down after an upset and helped you develop *self-regulation* as you got older. Sometimes, our earliest experiences might have been chaotic or unpredictable which can make self-regulation more difficult growing up. If you've had traumatic experiences, you might notice your ability to regulate develops more slowly or gets worse for a while.

If, for whatever reason, you are not able to self-regulate easily then it's a good time to mention the great news that your brain is a **fantastic plastic** brain! It's not actually made from plastic – we use this term because it behaves like plastic. It can adapt and change throughout our lives according to the environment it is in, something we call *neuroplasticity*. You can choose to be positive and feel happy whatever is going on around you. It's not always easy but you have the equipment in place, and I'm going to show you how to make the most of that equipment.

Nature or nurture

Scientists, psychologists and philosophers have been interested in why a human becomes the person they are for as long as people have been becoming who they are.

Nature - Some have argued that your personality is due to the way your brain is built in the womb and the wiring it develops there. They think it is influenced by genes and other biological factors. This is known as the nature argument, where your personality is seen as being innate, or fixed because of your biology.

Nurture - Others argue that your environment, experiences and the way you are raised combine to create your personality. This is known as the nurture argument where your personality is seen as being flexible as a result of your individual circumstances.

It is generally understood nowadays that both nature and nurture are important in your development. We definitely know that your brain responds and adapts to your environment because of brain scans called fMRIs (functional Magnetic Resonance Imaging) which have revealed all kinds of fascinating examples of this. The nature-nurture debate focuses on how much both these arguments influence your personality. No one yet knows the answer to this debate but maybe you have an opinion on it from your own observations?

One aspect of your personality is your *temperament*, or your ways of thinking, being and doing. Whichever way your temperament is formed, knowing about how it affects you can help you understand why you do or don't enjoy certain situations.

Introvert or extrovert?

The terms introvert and extrovert are often used to describe an aspect of a person's temperament, that is, how reserved (introvert) or outgoing (extrovert) you are. You're probably a mix of the two but have a look at these descriptions and see which you think best fits who you are.

It's not better to be an introvert or an extrovert – both temperaments are equally normal and equally valid! Around 1 in 3 people are introverts, while 2 in 3 are extroverts. Why not ask your adults which they think you are? You might be surprised how they see you. Feel free to check out how your friends see you and themselves too.

Introvert
Thinks about life and the world from the inside

☐ Needs to spend time alone to think and reflect

☐ Feels tired after socialising and needs to rest

☐ Enjoys thinking about ideas and how things work

☐ Prefers a few meaningful and close relationships to lots of casual ones

☐ Listens attentively to others

☐ Works out what they think before speaking about things

☐ Expresses themself well in writing

Extrovert

☐ Mainly interested by what's happening in the world around them

☐ Needs the excitement of being in social situations with others a lot of the time

☐ Feels tired and unmotivated when they spend too much time alone or thinking, prefers to be 'on the go' which is energising

☐ Loves to dive into things and learn by doing

☐ Prefers lots of friends and can fit in with different groups at different times

☐ Chatty and spontaneous

☐ May come across as confident, friendly, and assertive without having to think too much about what to say

☐ Expresses themself well verbally

"We are what we pretend to be, so we must be careful about what we pretend to be."

Kurt Vonnegut

Psychologists know that what you believe about yourself changes the way your brain works and has a powerful effect on how you feel, think and behave.

What do you believe about yourself? Finding out could help you to identify some of your biggest dots and as such, what you could use this book to help you work on in order to feel happier.

Below, scale your beliefs about yourself out of 10. One is as low as you can go, and 10 is pure zen.

Self-esteem

I don't deserve nice things or friends

I deserve nice things and friends because I'm a good person

1   5   10

Self-worth

I get everything wrong

I make mistakes sometimes, but I learn from them and keep trying. I don't have to get everything right to be important to others

1   5   10

Self-confidence

I like stick to what I know and don't like to try new things

I love trying new things

1   5   10

Self-image

I look awful

I'm happy with the way I look overall

1   5   10

Body image

I don't like my body

It's not perfect, but I love my body and the things it can do

1   5   10

World view

Nothing works out for me

I might do well, but if not 'you win some, you lose some'

1   5   10

Self-esteem is how you view yourself as a person and what you feel, think and believe about yourself and about how others think of you. Good self-esteem means you like yourself and think other people generally like you too.

Self-worth is what you feel, think and believe about your value to others and the world around you and the respect you deserve. Good self-worth means you feel you're someone with good qualities who has achieved some good things.

Self-confidence is how you act in the world because of what you see, feel, think and believe about yourself. Good self-confidence means you are sure of your abilities and value, even if there are things you can't do right now.

Self-image is how you see your overall appearance and what you feel, think and believe about it and about how others see you. Good self-image means you mostly like the way you look and can tolerate any aspects you're less happy with.

Body image is how you see your body and what you feel, think and believe about it and about how others see it. Good body image means you mostly like your body despite any parts you're less happy with.

World view is how you expect things to work out in your life and in the world around you. A positive world view means you are generally optimistic and hopeful.

Teenagers often love new experiences and trying out exciting or dangerous activities. Because of your system update, your judgment isn't always able to keep up with the desire for thrills stemming from your emotional brain. You may have been a very careful child who now takes risks which seem out of character. This will worry your adults and could be confusing for them and for you too. It's important to keep your thinking brain as engaged as possible when you notice this in order to reduce the risk to your longer-term wellbeing, both physical and mental. More on this later in Chapter Six, if you dare!

Think back over the past 48 hours. On a sheet of paper, list the different moods you've felt in that time. Include the positive ones as well as any that felt more negative. Tick the one(s) that felt the strongest to you.

Mood swings

Your brain is temporarily out-of-sync while it reorganises itself. The limbic system over-reacts because your pre-frontal cortex isn't yet up to date and isn't as good at being in control as it used to be, or as it will be in the future. Your brain makes chemicals to control your moods but doesn't always know how much of these chemicals to make now that you've got so many hormones floating about. This may mean you feel happy one minute and really sad, worried or angry the next, often with zero warning or reason. You might be bouncing with confidence at ten o'clock in the morning feeling invincible and like you've got everything sorted out, but also feeling like you always get everything wrong and have no friends by 10.01 a.m. This feels unsettling and can be bewildering for you and everyone around you. Your brain will learn in time and get the balance mostly right, and this will pass. Chapter Five will show you how to deal with these ups and downs while they last, through a wide range of relaxation and feel-good techniques.

Good stress vs bad stress

Short bursts of stress are rather good for your brain and body. The rush of adrenaline and cortisol that stress brings can improve your memory and make you more focused, energised, precise and creative. The problem comes when stress goes on for too long or happens too often (or both) causing the positive effects to disappear. You start to develop a worse memory, struggle to make decisions and feel overwhelmed, tired, agitated and upset. Sound familiar? It's important to recognise when stress affects you and take action to reduce it. You may become mentally unhealthy – or have a mental health problem – if it continues for too long. When something stresses you out, remind yourself that it will pass and there will be a time when you're OK again. Then make sure you have some ways to relax and recover. Skip ahead to Chapter Five if you need some stressbusting techniques in a hurry.

Fill in these sticky notes with the things you know give you good stress and bad stress. Try to find ways to cut out or reduce the bad stress from your life – you might want to speak to one of your adults if it feels out of your own control or if other people's demands on you are feeling too much.

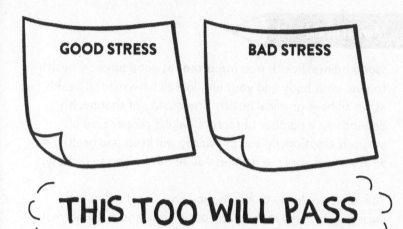

GOOD STRESS

BAD STRESS

THIS TOO WILL PASS

Stop, look and listen!
For some of us, it can feel more challenging to be able to notice our feelings. You may have trouble knowing if you feel sad, angry or any other negative or positive emotion. You may have always found it difficult to identify them or you may feel you've had to stop noticing them because things have been tough recently. You may find you feel odd or disconnected from your own inner sensations and perhaps even struggle to know if you are hungry or thirsty. As a result, you might find yourself forgetting to take good care of yourself – or even to go to the loo. Sometimes this is related to having a lot of stress or difficult circumstances to deal with. Sometimes you may just be so busy that your thoughts are taken up with whatever it is you're doing. If you find it tricky to know how you're feeling, every now and then, stop, look and listen – ask yourself what sensations you have going on, what thoughts you're aware of and what they might mean. And then have a drink of water!

Mental health

Good mental health is as important as good physical health to you, your body and your life. We all have mental health, as we all have physical health. The quality of that health depends on a number of factors. Taking proper care of yourself emotionally and physically will keep you healthy in all areas and improve it when you're not feeling so healthy.

You are more likely to experience emotional difficulties during your teens than at any other time and it is a normal part of growing up to have highs and lows, mood swings and intense emotions. Experiencing difficulties does not always mean you have a mental health problem. If you suffer from colds a few times a year, you probably wouldn't say you had a physical health problem so having a few tricky moments every now and then is not the same as having a mental health problem. However, those moments may be a warning to be kinder to your mind. If these difficulties persist and don't seem to clear up or keep coming back, that's when you might need to seek support and treatment to improve your mental health. Chapter Five will cover this in more detail.

A word of warning. Sometimes adults might believe that teenagers are selfish and only ever think about themselves. Socrates would have asked these adults a bunch of questions in order to understand why they believe that's true. Your adults might look at this book and wonder why I want you to spend even more time thinking about yourself. I'm not encouraging you to be selfish but in order to really know yourself, you do have to spend time working it all out. Neuroscientists are there to tell adults that self-understanding is essential in order to thrive. Add to that the fact that your brain is undergoing a system update and pruning itself to do better and be better, it makes sense to put the work in now while that brain is at the right stage of development to act on what you choose. And it definitely is work! Socrates worked every day at understanding himself. You're doing the same thing. You're a teenage philosopher.

 Go dotty!

In this chapter, you've had the chance to find out more about how your brain and body work and who you are as a person in your own right. Have you uncovered some more of your own dots? Add them here and keep working on joining them up to understand yourself more as you work through the book. Add more dots if you need to.

- E.g. I sometimes get really stressed without knowing why it's happening and feel sensitive when others criticise me.

- _____

- _____

- _____

Connect these dots – is it too early for you to name what
the whole picture is, yet? Don't get in a flap, it'll all become
clear in time...

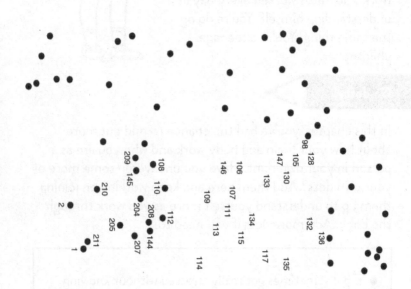

turn page on its side

The CHOOSE YOU! Process

NAME IT!

Now you've had the chance to think and **KNOW your SELF!**, is there a dot or something you've uncovered through this chapter that you'd like to **CHOOSE** to work on or change to help you be who you want to be? Perhaps something you think or believe, a habit you've formed, an instinctive reaction that bursts in too often, a thought you'd prefer to control or a repeated feeling you'd like to get on top of? You can now **NAME IT!** in the process grid on the next page. You could take a look at my example to see how it works, if you like.

You have enough boxes for up to five choices in the grid. Always keep to the same box number for each choice so you can track its progress as you use **The CHOOSE YOU! Process**. Feel free to flip through the book and track my choice to see how the process develops or check it out as you get to the end of each chapter.

I recommend you don't try to work on too many points at once – stick to one or two to start with. You can always come back to the grids after you've worked on each choice or made your change successfully. You'll be able to use the process as many times as you like. If you run out of blank boxes here, you could use sticky notes or a notebook to record your choices or use the spare grids at the back of the book.

I NAME IT!

E.g. I can be very sensitive and often get upset too easily by things people say.

1
2
3
4
5

In Chapter Three you'll learn how to **SHOW your SELF!** and **CLAIM IT!** which is the next step in **The CHOOSE YOU! Process.**

CHAPTER THREE

CLAIM IT!

SHOW YOUR SELF!

This chapter will:

1. Focus on the **CLAIM IT!** section of **The CHOOSE YOU! Process**

2. Help you understand why friendships and peer relationships become so important to you, in the real world and online, and why this sometimes causes conflicts with your adults

3. Explain why feeling excluded from situations or friendships and bullying hurt so much

4. Break down why you sometimes feel awkward, self-conscious, as though everyone is looking at you and like there's an invisible audience following you around 24/7

5. Lead on to Chapter Four

"People can tell you to keep your mouth shut, but that doesn't stop you from having your own opinion."

Anne Frank

Being seen and recognised as an individual in your own right is something your incredible brain-body has been especially programmed to claim during your teen years. You want to feel understood by those around you, and of course, by yourself. In fact, it's not just something  you want, it's something you've literally needed in order to survive. When you were a new-born baby, even without any words and special skills (and probably not much hair), you knew how to get yourself noticed, fed and looked after. You instinctively knew how to **SHOW your SELF!**

Born to connect

Since the moment of your birth, your brain has been developing its *cortex* to help you connect and communicate with others and become part of a social group. Even without trying, you have been learning to understand social situations and your own place in the group. For some babies and children, that group is a family and a culture. For others it might be a series of families and cultures. As you grew up, your instinctive brain worked out the rules of your group and you probably started to show less of yourself as you tried to fit in.

The neuroscience bit!

Some brains quickly develop a good understanding of social situations, making their owners confident in company. Some, especially neurodiverse brains, find this task much harder, leaving their owners feeling less confident in company. If you've experienced traumatic or sad events, your social understanding can be affected and take longer to develop but, as we've seen, your brain is an expert at adapting to your unique circumstances and learns from experience, and from observing other people. It usually takes until you are at least 25 years old for your brain to fully develop social understanding. Humans are complicated beings so it takes a while!

SOCIAL MEDIA enables people to show themselves to others in a way they can control, creating an ideal impression of who they are and what their life is like. It's like a shop window where all the best bits are displayed to attract as much positive attention and feedback as possible. That's great – who doesn't love a perfectly laid out collection of all your favourite things? It's important to recognise that what you see isn't a true reflection of people and their everyday life, whether they're your friends, *peers* or famous celebrities. Comparing yourself and your life to other people's often causes anxiety and is unhealthy.

Say what you see

How do you want to be seen by other people around you? Is that always the same, or does it depend on who is doing the seeing?

Write the things you'd like your family group to notice and understand about you on this Venn diagram in the left circle, what you'd like your friends to notice and understand in the right circle, and what you'd like them all to see in the middle where the circles overlap. Squeeze in as much info as you can. Some examples might be – *I'm kind*, *I care about the environment*, *I'm sporty*, *I'm into music*.

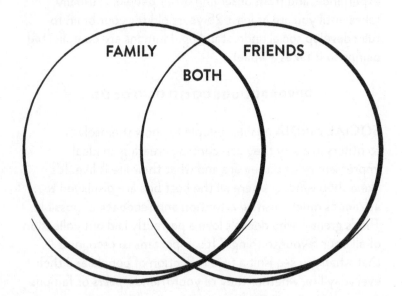

We know that the teenage brain works differently when you're with your friends and peers than it does when you're with your family group. It's more engaged and ready for action around your friends and keen to practise the rules of the new group, which will be different to the rules in your family group. Your Venn diagram will highlight where the differences show the most.

 The *anthropology* bit!

The thrive tribe

During adolescence, you need to feel, and be, understood in order to thrive. The instinct to connect that you were born with gets stronger and more adventurous, pulling you away from what's familiar and comfortable (and what is possibly a bit boring to you with all the other new and exciting options available to you). Your brain's now seeking rewarding new experiences, like-minds or a *tribe*. It craves a sense of belonging outside of the family group you've been part of and, in an ideal world, learnt to feel completely safe and 'at home' with. You are developing new likes and dislikes, needs and interests because your brain is scanning for signals from others and looking for social acceptance. Your social group starts to shift from your family and adults towards friends and peers, in real life and online, who are also trying to understand themselves with brains that are scanning for signals from you. You might leave old friends behind as you surge forward, or they may leave you behind as they take different paths. This can hurt so be as kind and understanding as you can be, and if it's happening to you, speak to your adults or other friends for support. Remember, it's not personal or because of anything you've done wrong.

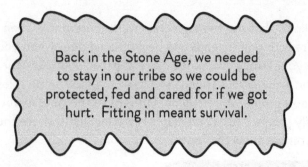

Back in the Stone Age, we needed to stay in our tribe so we could be protected, fed and cared for if we got hurt. Fitting in meant survival.

Two true!
To your adults, you're still so young and they feel that you need their care just as you've always done; to your teenage brain, you're ready to claim your independence and join (or lead) your own tribe. Like the Six Blind Scholars, you're each right and each wrong and you need to talk and work together, let go of your false certainties and reveal the whole truth using the truths you have to hand.

A note about your adults
It's not just you who was born with a social brain. Your adults have brains that need to connect and communicate too. When you pull away from them, they experience rejection and, as you'll see later in this chapter, that causes them actual pain. Cut them a bit of slack when they feel upset with you or if they say you're not grateful for everything they have done and still do for you. Every now and then, maybe ask them how it's all going for them. When you were little, you might have thought your adults knew everything but you're now beginning to see that they are just human, like everyone else, and can make mistakes or mess up too.

Temporarily conflicting programs
Seeing you searching for your tribe can leave your adults feeling sad and worried about you because they'll very quickly notice you're pulling away from them. You'll

probably spend more time trying to understand yourself and asking adults to understand you than you'll spend trying to understand them. When you know this, it's not hard to spot why there's potential for conflict. It's lucky you ended up with this book in your hands, isn't it? If you keep reading, the more you'll understand and be understood.

While you're all about new exciting experiences, the brains of your adults have reached a stage where they are programmed to seek stability and predictability. You'll experience very strong emotions that can get in the way of you understanding other people's intentions. Your ability to regulate your feelings is at an all-time low so it's likely your limbic system will perceive a criticism or threat in the way they look at you or their tone of voice, and overreact like a volcano to what were intended as everyday comments and actions.

Bridges in the hood
I often describe teenagerhood (if I may?) like standing on a bridge. Behind you is your childhood and all the things you used to enjoy. In front of you is your adulthood and the things you're becoming more interested in, some of which your adults won't understand or have any personal experience of. Sometimes you push forward while your adults are pulling you back – for example when you want to go somewhere or do something they aren't happy about and feel you're not ready for. Sometimes you're pulling back while your adults are pushing you forward – for example when they want you to take more responsibility or do homework and chores that you'd prefer to ignore. When you're both pulling or pushing at the same time in the same direction, that's when you are able to understand each other and yourselves.

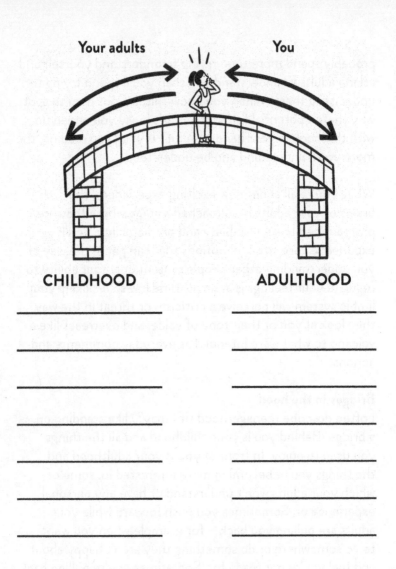

Your adults   **You**

CHILDHOOD   **ADULTHOOD**

_____   _____

_____   _____

_____   _____

_____   _____

_____   _____

Write under each pillar the things you used to like as a child, and the things you are interested in now.

When do your adults pull you back?

When do they push you forward?

Write examples you've had of this happening onto the diagram on the push and pull arrows. Think about why as well as when these things arise.

Win-win

Whenever there is conflict, it can feel like there has to be a winner and, inevitably, a loser. We call that win-lose. You might be desperate not to be the loser – and so is the other person (even if they're an adult!). This means disagreements can get out of all proportion to the situation that happened in the first place. Have you ever fallen out with someone and felt angry with them, but you can't remember what started it? That's what I'm talking about! If you can find a way to help you both feel like you haven't had to lose something, you'll make much stronger relationships and feel happier. Win-win is the way! Everyone loves a winner!

Finding your tribe

Your friends and peers are becoming extremely important to your need to belong somewhere (outside of your family group) and your brain wants you to spend as much time as possible in your new social groups. There are many reasons

why you might end up being friends with some people and not with others. You'll be looking for people who you feel 'get you', and who maybe share your way of thinking, as well as your ideas, beliefs or values – these friends are part of your tribe. You'll be influenced by other people's opinions and behaviour. You might identify yourself as part of a group because of your favourite music, teams, fashion, jewellery, books, films – and a hundred other things. Some people will seem exciting, some reassuring and some won't fit in as part of your tribe. Your tribe will keep changing and evolving as you go through life.

"I've learned that people will forget what you said, people will forget what you did, but people will never forget how you made them feel."

Dr Maya Angelou

We like to be with people who accept us, share our interests and make us feel good about ourselves. Being with friends is fun because they make you laugh, talk about things you care about, listen to your worries and advice, introduce you to new ideas, ask for your help and sometimes help you find solutions. They aren't in charge of you and they make you feel like you matter. It's possible that one or two of the friends you've already made might still be your friends in 50 years' time. I met my great friend, Charlotte, on the first day of secondary school 44 years ago and just this morning she popped in for a natter and a laugh. I told her I was writing this book for you and she made me promise it would be the kind of book we needed and would've wanted as teenagers. Paula, another school friend who rescues abandoned animals in California and nurses them back to health if they're sick, came over to see me after I had an operation recently. Who might be your golden friends when you're my age?

GOLDEN FRIENDS

Some of the people you are friends with now, or want to be friends with, won't feature further down the line as your ideas and preferences change and develop. There's a saying that friendships are *for a season or a reason*, and in my experience that's true. I was desperate to be Dawn's friend – she was funny and edgy. For one wonderful summer when I was 14, we hung out every day and had the best time. We never fell out or decided to stop being friends but once September came, we both happily went back to our different schools and I never saw her again.

Memory and motivation

Experiences you have during adolescence will shape your adult brain and you will still remember them well into your thirties. Your amygdala (Bob) and hippocampus in the limbic system are especially good at remembering emotional moments in adolescence and they adapt your brain to help you learn from them. When you're in a group of friends you feel comfortable with and connected to, your memory improves, you're much more motivated and you can learn more easily. When you're in a group that you don't feel comfortable with and you're feeling those strong ancient brain emotions, you'll find it really hard to learn anything because you will be alert to everything BUT the learning (you probably already know that from experience!). Why not show this book to your teachers, who may have forgotten what it was like to be a teenager? It might make your lessons even better if they are reminded.

"No one is too small
to make a difference."

Greta Thunberg

When you feel like you're an accepted part of your group, however large or small it is, you might find yourself becoming passionately involved in causes that matter to you, like protesting climate change or helping homeless people, or, well, anything that interests you! You may feel much more confident to **SHOW your SELF!** than you'd ever imagined. Be bold! You are more powerful than you know.

Buzz rewards

Have you ever been offered a reward by your adults for doing something you didn't really want to do? It probably worked and that's because the key to motivation for your brain is reward. Not all rewards have the same power though and your brain has its own ultimate system for rewarding you, called the *reward pathway*. During this period of intense social development, it gets a buzz every time you feel approval from your peers. The higher the regard you have for them, the bigger the buzz. You get this with your adults too, although it's not usually as strongly as with your friends. The buzz you get is from a chemical called dopamine and it feels great whenever it happens. Your emotional brain loves it when you're buzzing. You want more of it and it's hard to resist. Whilst your pre-frontal cortex is undergoing its system update, it isn't fully online to guide you and help you make good decisions or judgments. If you're a sensation seeker this can lead to risky behaviour – you may feel less inhibited and be less cautious and do things you usually wouldn't. You might find it harder to pay attention, plan, prioritise, organise yourself, complete tasks, understand other points of view, regulate your reactions and think about consequences – we call these important skills *executive functions* and they are significantly reduced when dopamine is buzzing around. This can happen anywhere in school, at home, at social gatherings – and might lead to problems if it gets the better of you. It's important to be aware of this so you can look out for the feeling and try to keep a level head

– something you can definitely do with practice.

Executive functions and emotional regulation don't fully develop until late adolescence so anything that makes them harder to use is a big disadvantage to your wellbeing.

Liking likes

It's this buzz that makes you enjoy the 'likes' and positive comments you read on social media. Every time there's a notification, you get that buzz. The more it happens, the more it motivates you. When you post something that gets fewer likes, you miss the buzz and feel disappointed and sometimes even sad. At this moment, you're more vulnerable to criticism, real or imagined, or to posting or sending something inappropriate to boost your numbers or get approval from a friend. Again, this is something you can be more in control of when you are aware.

Selfies are something that can become a problem because of those buzz rewards. You like to make yourself look fantastic (you're already fantastic!) and that makes you buzz. Then you want other people to approve and see how fantastic you are (they already know!), so you post it. You get the buzz again. Or you don't... if it doesn't get the likes!

Smart devices and gaming

Since your brain is fulfilling its adolescent mission and working hard to connect and communicate with the world, it's hardly surprising that you find it almost impossible to put your phone down for a minute or that you get upset/cross/angry/devastated/furious (delete as applicable!) when your adults won't let you use it (I'm right, right?). Your phone, and other devices, are the ultimate connection and communication tools and they're fantastic fun with huge learning potential thrown in – so why wouldn't you be glued to them? You get to be in control of how you relate to the world and others through them which is highly motivating and – yep – rewarding. It gives you that buzz from dopamine in your brain.

Devices can become addictive, literally, because dopamine is the chemical that drives addictions. You need to keep spending more hours using your device to maintain the same buzz. Keep an eye on your use of them – it's easy to spend all your spare, and not so spare, time attached to them. No one yet really knows whether this is damaging for you, your brain or your development because there haven't yet been any proper studies on it, but we do know that screen use can hijack the natural workings of your incredible teenage brain and affect the way it manages emotions. It also takes away time when you could be doing all the other things your brain needs like exercise, play, rest, sleep, other forms of learning and physical contact with your adults. If you begin to feel that you can't get through the day without your screens or it makes you angry to have to stop, talk to an adult and get support to reduce the amount of time you're spending on them.

Just as you can have misunderstandings with your adults, they'll also happen with your friends. Guaranteed. Disagreements can feel very painful because you rely on friends for your social contact and you become very attached to them. They can seem like the most important part of your life at times and falling out can seem catastrophic to you. Your friends will experience the same need for acceptance and approval and will have the same highly sensitive reactions as you do to other people's facial expressions, tone of voice and spoken or written words. You could take offence at things they say or do extremely quickly because you misread what they actually meant and things then blow up into a major falling out. Once you've got over the immediate reaction, you'll hopefully be able to listen to their explanations and say sorry if you need to. The same goes for them too, of course.

Falling out with friends is a natural part of growing up, but to be a good friend yourself you'll need to find ways to resolve problems when they arise. Not all friendships are healthy – see Chapter Six to learn more about when to let go of bad friendships.

Resolving friendship and family conflicts is going to be an important aspect of maturing. Not all adults are great role models for this – just watch the news and see how some politicians act and you'll see what I mean. Social media can almost seem to make it appear normal and acceptable to bear grudges and delight in bad behaviour during arguments but being able to work things out will make you happier in the long run and will mean you have more people to turn to when you need them.

TRUCE is a great mnemonic to help you with conflict resolution. You could learn it, try it, refine it, master it!

Talk it through, and listen too

Respect the other person's feelings

Understand everyone will have their own point of view

Compromise and negotiate to get a win-win outcome

Extend a gesture of friendship such as a smile, a hug (if welcome) and/or an apology

Friend zone
What kind of friend do you think you are? Add all your qualities as a friend to this checklist.

E.g. I cheer my friends up when they're upset

☐ _____

☐ _____

☐ _____

☐ _____

☐ _____

☐ _____

☐ _____

What one thing could you do to be a better friend?

_____

_____

_____

_____

_____

IN A WORLD WHERE YOU CAN BE ANYTHING, BE KIND.

All by myself ▶

Scientists have discovered that when you feel lonely, excluded, bullied or left out, the pain from your hurt feelings is as real as physical pain from an injury because the same brain pathways, or neural networks, are affected. This applies to every human, including your adults, and at your age it's the hardest it will ever be – studies have shown that your mood might drop and your anxiety increase, and these changes can worsen your self-esteem. Sometimes young people might even abandon activities they really enjoy or pretend not to like a less popular friend in order to avoid feeling or being left out or teased. Maybe that's happened to you?

It's the same story when you have FOMO (fear of missing out). You can worry that if you're not with the others when something fun happens, however small, you'll be forgotten and left behind. In other words, that this temporary situation of not being included will become a permanent state and you'll now be alone FOREVER! You might feel fearful that you'll never make another friend again but this isn't true – it's just a feeling that you get thanks to the Stone Age programming of your emotional brain. It's all an ancient safety device to keep you with your tribe to stay protected against the wild animals on your patch. However, in the modern world, *we can* be away from the tribe and survive. You can be missing from the action as a one-off or a series of one-offs and not be forgotten about or left behind. And you have more than one tribe that values you – your adults make up one of your tribes.

Permanent thinking
Think of time you were left out or couldn't go to an event that your friends were going to. What was it?

_____

_____

_____

_____

_____

_____

Remind yourself how you thought or felt about the situation – were you worried you'd be permanently left out from now on? Take control of that Stone Age thinking right now and teach your brain to switch to temporary thinking. Use this system and go from **PEG** to **TIS**

Permanent thinking is PEG:	Temporary thinking is TIS:
Permanent – I'll never be included in anything again	**T**emporary – I wasn't included this time
Extrinsic – This always happens to me	**I**ntrinsic – I can try to be included next time
Global – Everyone thinks I'm always boring	**S**pecific – Kai thinks I'm boring

Now you understand how your Stone Age brain causes these feelings, you can deliberately change your thoughts from permanent to emporary. Complete this chart next time you find yourself left out or unable to take part and turn your thinking around to show permanent thinking the wide open door:

Go from PEG to TIS

P _____ T _____

E _____ I _____

G _____ S _____

Alone not lonely
Spending some time alone is good for you as it helps your brain to process what's happened and learn from it. It's

important to learn to spend time alone and understand that this doesn't mean you are lonely.

Your wider identity may be fluid at the moment and can change many times (some aspects may feel more fixed – see Chapter Seven for more on this). Time alone helps you to feel comfortable and experiment in your own company with your emerging identity, trying it on for size and making adjustments. I went from ballerina to channel swimmer-in-training to a punk lurking around vinyl record shops, wearing a lot of black clothing and dodgy eyeliner, all in the space of about nine months (thanks, Dawn!). Your tribe will change too (sorry, Dawn!), often several times. Having a passionate interest in music that my parents couldn't stand (mostly The Cure!), and spending time alone to explore and develop my own identity led to me making two great new friends, Paul and Mustaq who were also fans of my favourite band (obviously I alone was the biggest fan ever!). We went to concerts and hung out in the school holidays, listening to cassette tapes (mostly The Cure!) and planning our meteoric rise to punk rock stardom. I changed direction several times and eventually withdrew my services from the music industry. But to this day, Paul still performs in bands playing all kinds of music (mostly not The Cure!).

If you react to being left out or bullied by withdrawing and isolating yourself for too long, it can affect how your brain develops and damage your confidence. Remember, you don't have to stay with an unhealthy tribe. Dust yourself off, decide which tribe suits you best and get back out there to **SHOW your SELF!** If that feels too difficult to do, ask one of your friends or adults for help or go to the resources section at the back of this book.

What about bullying? Falling out from time to time or getting cross with each other isn't bullying. Bullying is the deliberate and repeated use of power by a person or group to hurt or upset others. It doesn't have to be physical power. Bullying steals people's peace of mind and happiness. If you're being bullied, don't suffer in silence or shut yourself away. Ask for help. There are resources at the end of this book to support you. If you're worried you might be (intentionally or unintentionally) bullying someone else, there are resources at the back of this book to help you, too.

As a psychotherapist, I often hear young people talking about the popular group at school. It's tempting to imagine that the lives of its members are amazing. I can tell you for sure, even those who are seen as part of the popular group are going through the same things as everyone else. Remember that feelings aren't facts. Look for the evidence and other interpretations if you find yourself feeling on the 'outside'.

Awkward moments

There are so many reasons we sometimes feel awkward, listing them all is a bit, well, awkward.

Maybe you are shy and prefer to keep a low profile, or perhaps you're shy but really want to be seen and heard more. Shyness isn't always the same as unconfident or introverted, but it can make you feel awkward.

It's very common to go through a phase of being more

clumsy than usual which can make you feel awkward and self-conscious. Your body's growing and your brain's tied up with pruning so it's sometimes too busy to keep your body map up to date, meaning it doesn't always know exactly where in space your limbs, hands, feet, trunk and head are all of the time. You've also got new lumps and bumps growing that it hasn't had time to record the position of yet! You may find you use too much force in a movement, or not enough so you might knock into things or drop things more than you used to. The brain-body map will be updated when it gets a minute. Be patient with yourself.

Sometimes you can start to feel much more awkward and anxious around other people, even your good friends, especially in unusual or unfamiliar settings such as a new school or a new place, or going somewhere independently for the first time. Social situations can suddenly start to feel confusing and threatening and you might feel you can't cope without your adults around to support you. You may feel you don't know what to do or how to act and because of these feelings, your self-confidence and self-esteem might take a bit of a knock making you reluctant to meet up or hang out with others. Scientists believe that this is due to the emotional brain being super alert during the pruning phase, so it makes you worry more about how other people will react to you.

If this happens to you, you'll probably be interested in why it happens because if you understand it, you'll know how to deal with it, right? Well, it's all down to chemicals in your brain-body. The stress hormone, cortisol, is released making you more alert to the presence of others and especially to the idea of others watching or judging you, something we call *hypervigilance*. Worries start when you don't feel able to filter out normal feelings of fear, dread, anger or danger so your thinking brain (mis)uses its imagination to predict the unknown. It behaves like a fortune teller as if you already know terrible things will happen. It then starts coming up with a bunch of what ifs for you to worry about. Some of these might be 'what if I fall over', 'what if everyone laughs at me', 'what if I say something inappropriate' or 'what if I swear and shout'. There are other what ifs too. You know logically these what ifs are highly unlikely to happen but the thinking brain isn't able to reassure your emotional brain. I'll talk more about this in Chapter Five.

What ifs

List some of the what ifs that bug you. Decide honestly how likely they are to happen and tick the appropriate box. Ask someone to do this with you if you can't decide alone.

WHAT IF	Probably will happen	Might happen	Probably won't happen

Social anxiety

For some people, the sense of potential threat from other people's actions and reactions or from feeling watched and judged convinces the emotional brain that there's an overwhelming danger to you in social situations. This is often called *social anxiety*. The thinking brain, because it is underdeveloped until around the age of 25, cannot always help the emotional brain to calm itself and feel safe which leads to an instinctive fear response, similar to when you may have felt afraid of the dark as a young child. Social anxiety can be managed and improved with the right support, so if it's causing you upset or disrupting your confidence, try out some of the the pick'n'mix tips and techniques in Chapter Five. If the anxiety still persists, you may need to see your GP. Ask one of your adults to go with you. Take this book or your notebook with you if it will help you explain what you're going through.

The invisible audience

We know that the stress hormone, cortisol, acts on your brain whenever you are aware of your peers watching you. It makes you more aware of what you're doing and how you look doing it, compared to how other people look doing it, adding to the awkward feelings. You might make judgments and evaluate yourself and your body and focus on how it is the same or different from other people's bodies. You might feel self-conscious about aspects of your changing body that you haven't quite got used to yet and worry they are noticing or looking at those things, making you feel exposed and as though they can see everything you want to keep hidden.

For some young people, having peers sitting behind you in class can feel terribly uncomfortable and embarrassing because you're feeling so self-conscious that you worry they may be seeing parts of you that you can't check look OK. Because you've got used to making great efforts to control how you look to others to keep their approval and your status in the group, you might start to feel like everyone is looking at you all the time. Your brain can get into a loop so that it behaves as though your friends are always watching you, even when you're at home, on holiday or having a cuddle with your adults. This sometimes causes the feeling that you have an invisible audience around you, evaluating and judging you 24/7. It can stop you having fun and feeling relaxed. If you notice the invisible audience, try to remember what you learnt earlier in this chapter – it's not real. It's imaginary. Sure, it feels real but it isn't. Your brain is misusing its imagination to keep you safely in the tribe. But honestly, they can't see you making cookie dinosaurs with your little sister in your kitchen or whatever it is you want to do with yourself in the privacy of your own environment. Relax, it's going to be OK.

Hair, clothes, make-up, tech, trainers and other symbols of you and your tribe are things you may worry peers are going to notice, judge and evaluate, leading you to tightly control your appearance. Your adults don't always understand why you spend so long in front of the mirror, or why you perfect your selfies or feel desperate to buy the 'right' brands. Understanding why these things matter so much to you can help you try to keep them in balance while they're affecting you. They will become less important to you in time.

Hold on – it gets better

It's not just you! What you're feeling, going through and worrying about will be the same for your friends. They've all got it going on too. They're just as convinced that everyone's watching them and judging them as you are. Yes, even the popular ones – actually, especially them! So, guess what? That means that they are actually thinking about themselves, how they look, what people think of them and whether YOU can see everything they're trying to hide from view. They're probably not evaluating all those things about you that you feel so aware of at all. These feelings do start to fade as you get more comfortable with who you are. Keep going – you're doing great!

Go dotty!

In this chapter, you've learnt that you have a social brain that works differently depending on who you are with at the time. It is particularly sensitive during adolescence and learns from its environment and the people in it. Add any of your dots here that you've uncovered and keep working on joining them up to understand yourself as you read through the book. Add even more dots if you need to.

- E.g. I worry what other people think about me.

- _____

- _____

- _____

Get connected!

Connect these dots — can you claim to be able to unpack this section of the bigger picture, yet? Don't worry if not, just let it wash over you for now...

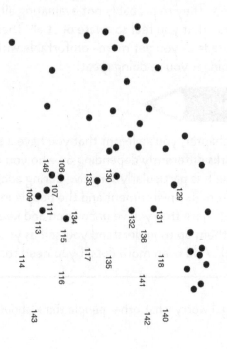

The CHOOSE YOU! Process

CLAIM IT!

Think or flip back to the end of Chapter Two and remind yourself what you found out in the **KNOW your SELF!** section and chose to focus on in the **NAME IT!** section of the process. Now it's time to **SHOW your SELF!** and **CLAIM IT!** as something that belongs to you, however helpful or unhelpful it is at the moment. It's yours and you are making it your own, your way, however **YOU CHOOSE**. Write what you are claiming into the process grid – see my example if it's not clear yet.

Remember – always keep to the same box number for each choice so you can track its progress as you use **The CHOOSE YOU! Process**.

If this chapter has given you something else to work on that didn't surface in the previous section, then **CLAIM IT!** now and add it to the next box down so you can use the process on that as you work through the book or come back to it later. For example, you might write *my imperfect body* or *my awkwardness* under **I CLAIM IT!**

I CLAIM IT!

e.g. Being sensitive is part of who I am at the moment.
1
2
3
4
5

Keep reading and find out in Chapter Four how to **GROW your SELF!** and to **REFRAME IT!**

CHAPTER FOUR

REFRAME IT!

GROW YOUR SELF!

This chapter will:

1. Focus on the **REFRAME IT!** section of **The CHOOSE YOU! Process**

2. Help you understand how and why the way you **CHOOSE** to view situations and your emotions affects how well you handle these and how you feel about them and yourself

3. Introduce you to the possibility of venturing outside your comfort zone and still feeling safe

4. Explain the conditions needed for you to **GROW your SELF!**

5. Develop your metacognition skills and show you how to grow your own neural networks

6. Break down the **Five Areas of Ambition**, and support you to identify yours

7. Lead on to Chapter Five

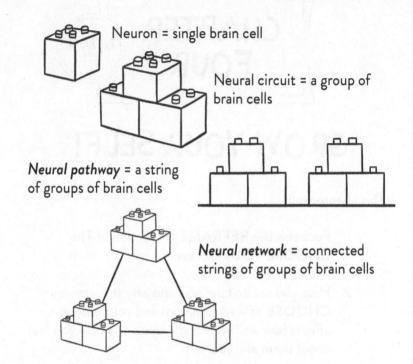

Neuron = single brain cell

Neural circuit = a group of brain cells

Neural pathway = a string of groups of brain cells

Neural network = connected strings of groups of brain cells

"One is not so affected by things that happen, but by the view one takes of them."

Epictetus

Epictetus (50-135 AD), another Greek philosopher, taught his students that whatever happens in your life, even if it's beyond your control, you can decide to look at it another way and handle it calmly. You are always responsible for your own actions and you can learn from the things you get wrong, and the things you get right.

I think he would've liked this chapter! In fact, he'd think it's **EPIC**... (sorry!).

But what does **REFRAME IT!** mean?

Well, it means what Epictetus said – to look at something in another way and from a different position. What might seem like a problem can be reframed and thought about with a different perspective in a way that is more helpful to you.

Take a look at this popular example you may have heard before:

How disappointing! It's almost all gone. I feel sad.

Brilliant! I've already had a good glug and I've still got some left. Life is great.

The facts of the matter don't change. There's the same amount of drink left in both glasses but we know that the half full way of looking at the situation grows new learning patterns, or neural networks, in your brain and literally lets you **GROW your SELF!** We call this way of thinking having a positive attitude. It improves your wellbeing, makes you more fun to be around and helps others to feel better at the same time. Maybe someone will even top up your glass for you as you've made them feel so great. Then you'll probably feel that the world is a rewarding place that treats you well which means you'll now have grown a positive world view to go with your positive attitude.

BLOOM WHERE YOU ARE PLANTED

We've already seen that wherever you grow up, you are part of (or planted in) an environment and culture. You don't usually have any say in what or where that is, but as Epictetus taught, you do have a massive say in what you CHOOSE to do with it.

The psychology bit!

Lev Vygotsky, a psychologist born in Belarus in 1896, studied how the environment and culture around young people affects how you grow, develop and learn. His work is still used today to train teachers, as it was when I trained to be a teacher, too (that was NOT in 1896, thank you!). Vygotsky found that *you learn in the context of the social world you are part of*, and the relationships you have with people are amongst the most important influences on your learning. You'll remember that we talked about that idea in the last chapter.

Comfort zone

Vygotsky was one of the first scientists to write about the idea of a comfort zone. You probably know what that is already. When you are comfortable doing things that are not particularly challenging and don't really push you, we say they're in your comfort zone. People often like to stay in their comfort zone because it's, well, comfortable! It feels safe so it's good to spend time there but stay there all the time and you'll start to feel, and be, a bit stuck.

He taught us we have another two zones to deal with:

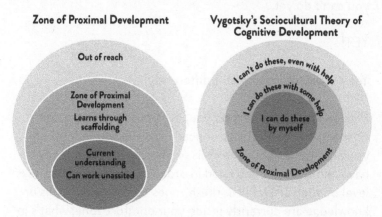

The furthest zone is where there are things that would be too difficult for you to learn because you don't yet have the physical, intellectual or emotional skills to be able to manage it.

YET. Did you notice that tiny word I slipped in there?

The middle zone, the *Zone of Proximal Development (ZPD)*, is where you can't quite get to by yourself **yet** but with the right support, you can begin to try it out and then master it. You'll need an adult or a peer who can manage the task already to guide you. I'd bet my vinyl punk records that if you've ever been taught anything by a friend, maybe the rules of something you enjoying playing, hacks for a video game, the latest dance craze or song lyrics, you've learnt it superfast? That's because you learn in the **context of the social world you're part of** and... sorry, I'm repeating myself!

Now you've mastered learning in the ZPD, you can get to those things that were once in the furthest zone. You've grown the neural networks in your brain, so your zones will shift again and now the furthest zone has new things in that you can't do yet.

YET!

Yet = a way of looking at it differently!

Pick an area that interests you, like your favourite game or sport, creative activity or academic subject or anything you like. Think about the skills or knowledge you already have and the skills you need in order to progress to the next level of your ZPD. Fill in these zones to show what skills or knowledge are currently inside your comfort zone, what's in your ZPD and what's in your future ZPD.

Zone of Proximal Development

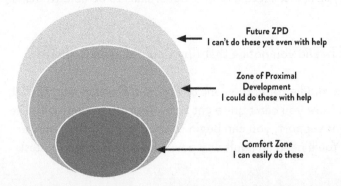

Future ZPD
I can't do these yet even with help

Zone of Proximal Development
I could do these with help

Comfort Zone
I can easily do these

Can you work out what help or support you need to make it to the next level? Once you're there, you could draw this diagram again, update it with what you've achieved and what's now in your comfort zone, and plan a new ZPD and future ZPD.

> "Whether you think you can, or you think you can't - you're right."
>
> **Henry Ford**

Henry Ford is credited with saying that whatever you think about your own ability to do something, you'll make it true. So, if you believe you're rubbish at something or convince yourself that you'll never be any good at it, you'll end up being right. Your confidence and self-esteem will drop and your neural networks won't grow in a way that would be useful for mastering whatever it is you're busy saying you're so rubbish at. We call that a *self-fulfilling prophecy*. Then, when you make a mistake or mess up - which you will, because all humans make mistakes and mess up as part of the learning process – you can use it to prove your false certainty. See the next page for an example.

You:
I'm rubbish at maths. I'll never be any good at it.

I messed up my maths test.

See, I told you I was rubbish at maths!

Dr Sharie:
Yep, it's 'cos you're an amphibian. Frogs don't count!

What would Socrates do if you sat and had this conversation with him? Yes, he'd ask you a load of questions to break down your false certainties. Because false is what they are. If you've ever surprised yourself by doing something you weren't sure you could do, you'll know that already. Your brain-body **wants** you to succeed and will do its best to help but it needs you to believe in yourself in order for it to grow the right connections.

What if we take that self-fulfilling prophecy and **REFRAME IT!** so we start to look at it another way?

Write on the sticky note a time when you achieved something you never thought you'd be able to. It can be anything at all. I've done mine to spur you on!

Thankfully, the first part of what Henry Ford said is also true. If you believe yourself to be capable of something, or that you'll be able to do it in the future, then you'll start to grow the neural networks to make it happen. You'll need to work in your ZPD to get there and keep the networks growing but, trust me, you'll get there if you try.

The biology bit!

Expect the best when you tackle something challenging because you will improve your chances of making it work out well. What you believe you can learn or do creates the right environment in your brain-body to make it happen. Lots of sports professionals already use this approach when getting ready for their training and events. It works with learning as well. By visualising yourself succeeding, you're helping to prepare your neural networks for growth. Of course, you do still have to put the work in. Believing you'll do well in the test will take you some of the way and give you a kickstart, but you must do your bit to make the most of the new neural networks waiting to soak up whatever you need to learn or do. Learn with a trusted adult, good friend or group of friends you feel comfortable with and you'll bloom. If you're someone who prefers to learn by yourself, you can deepen your understanding and ability to use what you've learnt by explaining it to and discussing it with others, whether face to face or via tech.

All dogs are... Thankfully, I've taught you that all dogs are mammals – I know you thought they were amphibians for a while but no, you got that wrong! Lucky I was there to put you straight, right? And you're a mammal too (I know you knew that), but not all mammals are the same. They've each adapted to their environment, just like you have. Don't make like a whale and believe you can swim underwater for two hours without surfacing for air – you can't. That goes beyond the power of belief! **Stay within the laws of science and physical possibility and it will be achievable!**

Growth mindset

When you **REFRAME IT!**, you look at things another way.

What if your personality, social skills, creativity, intelligence and physical ability are not fixed but can be grown and improved throughout your life? That's the thinking behind a growth mindset: it's when you **CHOOSE** to keep growing your neural networks to achieve your ambitions in life.

Fixed or growth?
If you were playing a video game and you couldn't get beyond level two, what would you say and do?

SAY	DO	SAY	DO
I can't do it	Give up	I can't do it yet	Work out a way to improve your skills
	Fixed mindset		Growth mindset

Your answer will tell you what you need to know!

Write one thing that you can't do now that you'd like to be able to. Keep it within the laws of science and physical possibility!

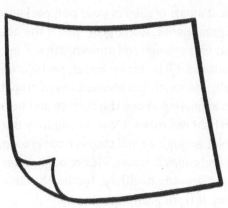

Can you look at it differently? How could you **REFRAME IT!** to turn it from a negative into a positive?

Write it here with a different focus. (Hint, if this is tricky, try adding YET to your sentence and see if that helps).

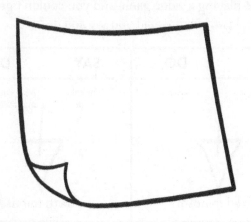

The botany bit!
Do you know what conditions are needed to successfully grow a plant?

Seed   Soil   Light   Air   Water

Even the most amazing seed in your pot, packed with energy and great genes, won't grow well if the conditions are not right. Not enough soil underneath will mean it can't steady its roots so it'll be blown about, perhaps unable to support itself. Too much soil above it might stop its earliest shoots from appearing above the surface and being noticed. Not enough light will make it lose its vibrancy due to lack of energy. Not enough air will stop it from growing and developing, and cause it stress. Not enough water will dry it out and stop it growing healthily. Too much water will rot the roots and stop it from growing.

Other needs
Your plant needs the right temperature for growth as well
as protection from frost, wind and being crushed – amongst
other things.

You're not so different...
What would happen if your conditions were out of balance
and you didn't have enough of some things and too much
of others? Let's see what the effects on your growth,
development and happiness would be. For each plant
problem identified in the following sentences, check the grid
on the next page to see what there'd be too much or not
enough of for YOU to thrive:

- Not enough soil underneath (so for you, that's
  support from your adults, home, environment and
  culture) will mean it can't steady its roots so it'll be
  blown about, perhaps unable to support itself (so for
  you, that means you'll feel insecure and won't have
  much self-confidence).

- Too much soil above it might stop its earliest shoots
  from appearing above the surface and being noticed.

- Not enough light will make it lose its vibrancy due to
  lack of energy.

- Not enough air will stop it from growing and
  developing, and cause it stress.

- Not enough water will dry it out and stop it growing
  healthily.

- Too much water will rot the roots and stop it from
  growing.

Seed	Soil	Light	Air	Water
genes	your adults	love	learning	friends
neuroplasticity	home	safety	challenges	hobbies
hormones	environment	rest	opportunity	fun
brain-body	culture	exercise	reframes	nutrition
energy	support	sleep	mindset	relaxation

Other needs

You need the right emotional temperature to grow in – so you'll need some good stress to fire you up and motivate you, but not too much! You'll also need the right amount of protection from bullying, danger and disease.

Where are the gaps in your conditions? Do whatever you can to keep the balance right and find ways to limit or close any gaps. Talk to someone about this if you have lots of gaps, or check the resources page for help. Remember, your incredible brain will always adapt to your circumstances to help you survive them, but give it all the help you can to thrive and flourish by improving your growth environment.

Epigenetics

In an unhealthy environment, some of your helpful genes switch off and some of your unhelpful genes switch on. In a healthy environment, some of your helpful genes switch on and some of your unhelpful genes switch off. You are not a

pre-determined end product – you are a seedling with the
potential to become incredible. And happy.

〇ꝺ〇ꝺ〇ꝺꝺ〇ꝺꝺ〇ꝺ〇〇ꝺ〇ꝺ〇〇ꝺ〇〇ꝺ

You'll need a reason to want to grow, which means having a
sense of purpose, or as I like to call it – an area of ambition.
I'll cover the **Five Areas of Ambition** shortly – keep reading!
You'll also need the belief that you can keep growing.

Decide what you need to **GROW
your SELF!**, flourish and truly
bloom where you're planted. Try
to pick things you can provide
with the right support and then
use this book, and other support
systems, to work on adding them
into your life. Your needs will be
unique to you.

Examples might be: books, time to
train, self-belief, courage, confidence.

Into the dark
It's not really possible for plants to get too much light and
that's where we humans are different. Tech screens give
off a lot of light (often at the wrong time of day) which
can be too much for your brain to cope with, affecting its
preparations for the next day. Research suggests that in
the hour or so before bed, screen light confuses your brain
stem's circadian rhythms (awareness of day and night) and
can prevent you getting to sleep and sleeping well. General
advice is that we should all wind down without screens for at
least an hour before you go to bed. If you need something

to help you relax, why not listen to a meditation, do some yoga or turn on an audiobook? We know that your brain-body needs darkness for proper rest and sleep and to enable it to metabolise, process learning, store memories, heal and clear itself, refresh and reset overnight.

Screens themselves **haven't** been shown to be directly damaging and we know they are a great addition to your life, so I'm not suggesting you stop using them! Some screen time will enhance your life and boost your learning. But too much screen time might hamper your efforts to **GROW your SELF!** if it hijacks your neural networks. It's all about the balance.

Research is showing us that too much gaming and computer use can contribute to a jumpier mind which races around rather than focuses in depth on things. This causes a lower ability to concentrate for lengths of time and worse *working memory*, which is the space you have in your mind to remember what you need to be doing at the same time as you're doing it.

We've also seen that dependency on screens can develop thanks to our dopamine buzz system. You might call this screen addiction. You could experience worse sleep and find it especially difficult to get to sleep (which is usually harder for teens already), or notice more depressive symptoms, poorer executive functioning and exhausting levels of hypervigilance. Use the glossary if you don't remember what any of those terms means from earlier in the book.

To grow your neural networks, your growth conditions need to be in balance. With good conditions in place, you'll be able to view everything that comes your way as an opportunity to learn something or as a challenge rather than something that feels uncomfortable because you might not be able to do it. It's all about how you **REFRAME IT!** Metacognition is a great mind fertiliser.

Fertiliser gives plants and crops extra nutrients to help their health and resilience. A bit like eating your five-a-day fruit and veg does for your body.

Remember what metacognition is?

Yep, it's thinking about your thinking.

Remember who encouraged it?

Correct! Socrates. And me, I encouraged it, too. Oh, and loads of other philosophers. And plenty of books.

"I know that I know nothing."

Socrates

The best place to start with metacognition is to know that you have so much to learn. Not because you're a teenager. I'm not suggesting you need to be better. Nope – it's because you're a human and we all have so much to learn because knowledge is infinite. I was in my thirties when I suddenly realised how little I knew. Before that, it felt really important to keep persuading myself and everyone else that I knew loads. Maybe that's how it feels for you? Or maybe you already feel like you know nothing and it worries you? Don't let it worry you – if it was good enough for Socrates, it's good enough for us.

Growing your neural networks is all about making connections in your learning by thinking about your thinking. It's a natural process that your brain carries out all the time anyway, so this is just about doing it on purpose. It's a bit like getting to meet your friend's friends, then their friend's friend's friends. That's how you grow a network.

Learning to learn
Any learning skill you master in your life works the same way. The more you use the network involved, the better it gets, the faster it works and the longer it lasts. Your brain will superglue the network to make it automatic and preserve it for as long as you need it. **Use it or lose it!**

The maths bit!
Let me give you an example. When you were learning your number bonds to 10, you had to remember the pairs to make the whole number, 10:

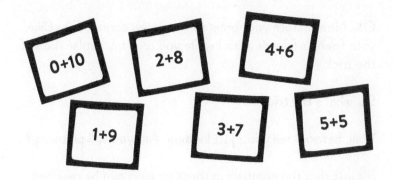

If one of your adults had shown you 'the trick' at this point, you wouldn't have had to learn any more bonds, whether to 10, 500 or to 9,000,000,000,000,000 because after these they're just a variation on the same theme.

So what's **the trick**?

Before I tell you, read the quote from Carol Dweck, a psychology professor who has studied and written about growth mindsets:

"Picture your brain forming new connections as you meet the challenge and learn. Keep on going."

Carol Dweck

OK. Now picture your brain forming new connections (like your friend's friends again) while you read my explanation of the trick.

So, what's **the trick**?

Well, before I tell you... just kidding! Are you still picturing?

It's just that the numbers in these six pairs can be reversed to complete the bonds. That's all you need to learn. And you can then apply them to tens, hundreds, thousands and so on. Your brain spots the pattern and matches it in similar situations or with similar problems. Do it a few more times and you'll start to remember them automatically as the neural networks get embedded in your brain.

0+10	10+0
1+9	9+1
2+8	8+2
3+7	7+3
4+6	6+4
5+5	5+5

It's all about patterns and your brain has already been learning through spotting and linking patterns since you were born. The more patterns it spots, the more it looks for them, the more it matches them, and the more it learns. Clever, eh? It's not just maths patterns either – patterns are everywhere. In spellings, sounds, games, music, art, nature, space and everything else you could think of.

How do I do metacognition?
A great technique is to take a third position. Not in the ballet sense, though!

When you're learning or talking to someone, instead of seeing things from inside your own head, or inside the other person's, imagine stepping outside yourself and stand alongside, observing, thinking and asking questions as if you're Socrates (or anyone you want). Sometimes it's easier to imagine yourself watching it on screen or from above. You won't always be able to do this at the actual time because you may be using a lot of your brain power to start with, although it gets easier with practice because you'll have developed the networks you need! It might feel weird to start with, trying to manage a conversation at the same time as observing. Practise as often as you can in short bursts and you'll soon be building those neural networks!

Reverse metacognition
You already know your brain has neuroplasticity – that's why it can do all this network stuff and grow itself, adapting to the environment and to what you're learning. It's great! However, it's also why your brain does some of the less helpful stuff too. Like troubling you with stuff.

When it makes life difficult, it's simply trying to adapt itself and make a pattern match to a previous situation. It automatically repeats what worked, even if that was something that caused you to feel scared, upset, angry or anything else. The good thing is that your brain can be taught to learn new ways and adapt differently. That's all in Chapter Five.

> # "One life is all we have, and we live it as we believe in living it."
>
> ## Joan of Arc

What if I'm just not very clever?

As a former teacher, I don't believe in *not very clever*. Every young person I've ever taught was clever. Even the ones who'd never been told and who definitely didn't think it was true. And when I told them they were clever, and showed them the evidence, they went on to be even cleverer.

I once worked with a little human who told me he wasn't clever. He was six years old and I was heartbroken to hear him say those words because it meant that at such a young age he'd written off his chances of ever doing well. His mum told me they were all a bit rubbish at school in her family. He was quiet and reserved in class but flew around like a rocket at playtime, leaping over obstacles or around other children and he never collided with any of them. Indoors, he kept his head down and himself out of trouble. It would have been easy to not notice him. Except I did notice him. Maybe it was because he reminded me of myself at his age, or maybe it was the contrast between his confidence outside the classroom and inside it. This stuff fascinated me.

He could just about write his name but was very reluctant to write anything else. By which I mean he wouldn't. OK, couldn't. One day, I sat on the floor with him under the table where he was taking refuge from the overwhelming job of writing a sentence with the word 'big' in it. I said I'd seen him on the playground, sprinting with the speed and balance of a sleek cheetah. I wondered why he always wanted to make himself seem small in the classroom. That's when he told me he wasn't clever. No one in his family was clever, he said. I told him that running really fast and never bumping into anything was clever, but he didn't believe me. He said it was easy and anyone could do it. I showed him that I (genuinely) couldn't do it. I explained that his brain-body knew how to move instinctively around anything that was in his way. He was super smart and could do something his teacher would love to be able to do but couldn't. How great would it be if he could use that same skill with his writing? He looked at me as if I'd lost my marbles but I asked if it would help to try writing on huge bits of paper with a toy cheetah attached to his pencil, swerving it around and between dots I'd drawn on the page, just like he did on the playground. He nodded so we tried that. The dots formed letters, and the letters formed words, and the words made a sentence when we lined up the pieces of paper across the hall floor.

It took about three weeks of doing this for 15 minutes every day (but never during his playtime because that was when he felt competent and this was essential for keeping up his confidence) before he and his mum brought me two pages of writing he'd done at home over the weekend. He said he felt big now he could write more than just his name. I'd be lying if I didn't tell you all three of us were in tears. He'd been paying attention since Reception but had never felt able to work out what to do with what he knew – it had felt much too scary and risky to try. I just needed to translate, or reframe, writing into something that made sense to him and something he knew he could do, and let his brain connect it to what he already knew how to do so well. He grew his own neural networks and went on to love writing, sometimes even at the table rather than under it. He always loved zooming around like a rocket more, though. He was proof that you can learn new things but still be your own unique self.

School

Perhaps the most important part of learning is a willingness to make mistakes and sometimes this is a huge challenge to the teenage brain because of the sensitivity it feels to being watched or coping with the invisible audience. Sometimes, hearing a teacher call your name can make you blush and feel horribly self-conscious as you feel everyone is looking at you. The thought of making a mistake under this pressure is deeply uncomfortable and can leave you unwilling to engage in lessons as fully as you could, or even prevent you from learning due to your emotional brain blocking your thinking brain from functioning efficiently. If you experience any of these difficulties, it's a good idea to speak to someone to help you manage your stress and anxiety. If you can reduce your overall stress, these experiences can be reduced as well. Chapter Five has some great hacks to calm an over-stressed brain.

As we've already seen, you will generally learn best in a social setting with motivation that comes from your emotional brain's needs being met. Learning from, and with, your peers and friends can provide some of the richest, most memorable learning experiences that will stay with you long into the future and deepen your brain's connections. For most young people that happens in school. Learning situations are all different and some people prefer to learn by themselves, perhaps because of the anxiety that the brain is experiencing during this pruning phase. You may be learning at home or in places other than a school because of your anxiety or for another reason – remember to connect your learning with your emotional needs if this is your situation and discuss what you're learning with your adults or friends.

What you learn in school or home-school can be great fun or really stimulating if you enjoy the subjects, but that's not always the case across the whole curriculum. You may find some subjects harder than others. That's not because you're not good enough, but because your brain has preferences or makes sense of some things more easily than others. Because you're unique!

"Remember to look up at the stars and not down at your feet. Try to make sense of what you see and wonder about what makes the universe exist. Be curious. And however difficult life may seem, there is always something you can do and succeed at. It matters that you don't just give up."

Stephen Hawking

Be curious

We all have a world view that is individual and specific to us. Yours will frame how you see yourself, the things, good and less good, that happen to you and around you, and what sense you're able to make of them. Your world view grows out of several powerful influences, including your family's world view, your cultural background, experiences you've had and your close relationships. It's all too easy to become stuck with only the one view of the world you're living in, from a window that's in need of a proper spring clean or could do with having the curtains pulled back. The quality of your window can seriously limit how you see your future and what you are capable of. Be curious! Being curious means that you try to understand and explore ideas and questions about your life. It also means you reflect on feelings, thoughts and actions instead of immediately jumping to definite answers. Curiosity opens your mind to other truths and helps you to **REFRAME IT!** What if you could grow your neural networks on purpose to look outside of your normal view or even from a different window frame completely? Keep going. It's time to explore your universe more deeply by thinking about your own ambitions.

Ambition

What does this word, ambition, mean to you? You might link it with a desire to be super successful and for some people that is exactly what ambition is. But for many people, it just means a desire to do or achieve something. It doesn't have to be becoming the next Mo Salah, Dani Dyer, Malala Yousifazi, Usain Bolt, Greta Thunberg, Chris Packham, Caitlyn Jenner or Albert Einstein. Your ambition might be to swim the English Channel but it might as easily be to make a difference to someone you know who is having a hard time, planning a trip to New York, mastering a revision plan, taking part in a try-out or learning to code. Ambition is whatever it means to you.

The Five Areas of Ambition

You may never have considered this, but learning doesn't have to be restricted to what others determine you should know or do. It doesn't have to be something passive or done sitting down. You can identify your own learning goals and be curious about what might lead you to develop an **Area of Ambition**. Feeling competent in an area of your life is important to keep your confidence growing and to give you courage to take bold leaps that can really pay off for you. This can help keep you focused on your own goals when it's hard to stay motivated in subjects you're less inspired by. Perhaps you already have an interest, but maybe you've never stopped to think of it as an **Area of Ambition** before. Hobbies, personal pursuits and out-of-school activities can drive your choice of ambition and are all valid options. Or maybe you don't already have an ambition and the idea is making you curious? Stay curious!

When you know what really motivates you and you feel passionate about learning for what you want out of it, school work can become more meaningful and you can connect the dots from your learning to this bigger picture. You can view anything you learn, even if it's not interesting to you, as giving you more dots towards what you ultimately want to do, know or find out. You'll grow new connections and you will be able to link your school studies to your own sense of purpose. As well as simply enjoying yourself in the moment (which is as good a reason as any to do something), you might find that identifying your **Area of Ambition** can help you see yourself as the future adult version of you who is pursuing a path that means something to you and inspires you. You might have ideas about your future career if you've started to think about that already, but it could just as easily be to do with deeply personal ambitions and challenges that you want to do for the fun and sense of achievement. Whatever your individual motivation, it will help you to make connections with your learning and feel more inspired, more competent and more confident. As I've mentioned, an area of ambition doesn't have to be something you want to excel in or be the best at – but it can be. What matters most is that it's something you feel driven to do and something that gives you pleasure and a sense of achievement.

The **Five Areas of Ambition** are not presented in any particular order because they're all of equal value:

1. **Artistic** – dance, painting, drawing, writing, anything creative

2. **Altruistic** – caring for others, spiritual interests, social, compassion

3. **Athletic** – any form of physical activity using your strength, co-ordination and physical skills

4. **Academic** – learning, and applying learning, in any area of interest from astrophysics to learning itself

5. **Alternative** – anything that isn't covered in the previous categories such as travelling somewhere interesting or exciting, becoming vegan or a million other possibilities...

If you decide to take up this **Area of Ambition** challenge, there is no restriction to keep to one area – but make sure you really focus on whatever you decide on as your area or areas. Then pin down what specifically you want to do or achieve within that area. Or, start with the specific ambition or goal and see which area it falls into. As with most things in life, some of your goals may well involve more than one area. You may also find that once you've explored an area, you go on to develop it further with something new, or you might move to an entirely different interest and area. Anything is possible!

Now over to you.

What are your goals and dreams? Which area are you going to choose? And what specific aspect of that area are you going to develop just because you want to? If you already know what your burning interest is, go ahead and decide. Then go for it and give it all you've got. Who knows where it could lead you?

Need more help deciding? Consider these questions to help you narrow down the field a little.

> What are you already good at, generally and specifically?

> Who inspires you?

> Why do you want to achieve this thing?

> What prevents you at the moment from achieving your goals?

> If you had a spare four hours today what would you choose to spend it doing?

> What have people said they admire about you?

> What do you need to do to be able to achieve your ambition?

What challenges might get in your way?

What qualities or skills do you have to support you?

Who could help you?

Where could you find out more about the things that interest you?

Record your ambition or ambitions and tick them once you've achieved your goals.

My Area of Ambition	✔

When the going gets tough...
Challenge is part of everyday life and everyone has things to face or do that they'd prefer to avoid or ignore. When you recognise your own fearful feelings but go ahead, do it anyway and conquer whatever it was that made you fearful, you can accomplish things you never thought you'd be able to. You know what causes the fear because you've met Bob and you also know why they want to keep you safely in your comfort zone. Sometimes Bob is more scared of you succeeding than failing, although you won't always know that's what's going on. If you succeed, Bob will worry you'll keep doing it and then they'll have to work even harder to keep you safe. But Bob learns from experience and by conquering the fear and doing

it, Bob will learn that you're safe and will stand down. If you take up challenges in your Area of Ambition, which is chosen by you, for you, and led by you for your own pleasure and pride, you can find out things about yourself you'd never have imagined possible.

Bob – the part of your limbic system that makes you fearful. Bob makes a proper debut in the next chapter, so watch out for that name!

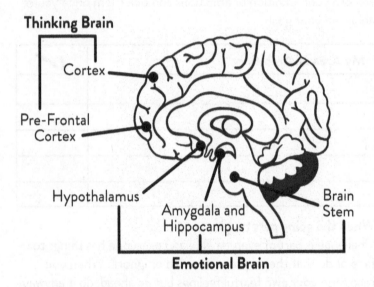

Thinking Brain

Cortex

Pre-Frontal Cortex

Hypothalamus

Amygdala and Hippocampus

Brain Stem

Emotional Brain

The Change One Thing challenge
Challenge yourself to do one brave thing that scares you in the next week. It doesn't have to be a huge thing like a bungee jump (but it can be)! It might be something like talking to that new person in your class, answering a question you're not sure you've got right or... whatever!

If it doesn't work out the first time, or you lose your nerve, just keep trying until you get there. Write it down if you want to and give yourself a big tick when you achieve it. Then keep setting yourself Change One Thing challenges.

ONE BRAVE THING

"Fall seven times, get up eight."

Japanese proverb

... the tough crack on!
Resilience means having the courage, capacity and confidence to keep trying when things are tough, and to recover from challenges. You'll need some downtime after a challenge to let the dust settle. This will enable your network to adapt to what it has taught you. Relaxation and hanging out with people you love and who love you rebuilds your power to try again. Then, the best way to increase your resilience is to approach the next challenge with an open mind and determination. And repeat.

Asking for help is a great way to grow your resilience networks. Completing **The CHOOSE YOU! Process** will get you there too, so it's lucky you're here!

"Become what you are."

Friedrich Nietzsche

The next chapter will show you ways to grow your resilience and help you become your version of you.

Go dotty!

In this chapter, you've learnt how to manage the way you think about things and the reasons why it's important to do so in order to flourish in your life. You've also read about the conditions you need to create to keep growing your neural connections so they're as helpful as possible. Add any of your newly discovered dots here and keep working on joining them up to understand yourself as you keep working through the book. Add more dots if you need to.

- E.g. I sometimes give up on things too easily.
- _____
- _____
- _____

Connect these dots – can you run with looking at the puzzle in a different way, yet? You'll get there faster if you do...

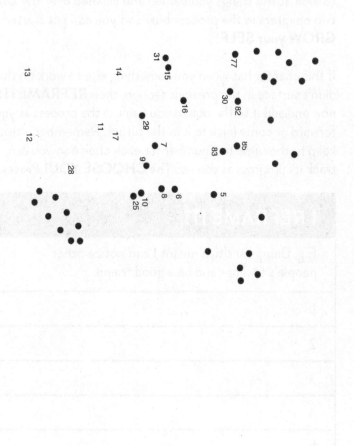

The CHOOSE YOU! Process

REFRAME IT!
It's time to **REFRAME IT!** Write the new ways you're going to look at the things you named and claimed over the last two chapters in the process boxes so you can get started and **GROW your SELF!**

If this chapter has given you something else to work on that didn't surface in the previous section, then **REFRAME IT!** now and add it to the box so you can use the process as you go forward or come back to it in the future. Remember - always keep to the same box number for each choice so you can track its progress as you use **The CHOOSE YOU! Process.**

I REFRAME IT!

E.g. Being sensitive means I can notice other people's feelings and be a good friend.
1
2
3
4
5

Keep reading and find out in Chapter Five how to **HELP your SELF!** and start to **TAME IT!**

CHAPTER FIVE

TAME IT!

HELP YOUR SELF!

This chapter will:

1. Focus on the **TAME IT!** section of **The CHOOSE YOU! Process**

2. Break down why emotional reactions can feel overpowering and out of control

3. Introduce you to **Bob** and the different responses the brain can have to emotional threats

4. Explain the Stone Age survival mechanism of **freeze, fight, flight**

5. Reveal a pick'n'mix menu of techniques for you to use in order to **TAME IT!**, upgrade and retrain Bob to get you back in control and **HELP your SELF!**

6. Identify mental health conditions and when to seek professional help for problems that keep returning or won't go away

7. Lead on to Chapter Six

As humans, we are prone to seeing anything that gets in our way of feeling safe and happy as a problem. We like to feel comfortable, chilling in our zone. The previous chapter helped you to look at things differently and **REFRAME IT!** This chapter provides you with loads of ways you can **HELP your SELF!** and **TAME IT!** Whatever it is that needs taming, the tips and techniques in this chapter will help you so you can **CHOOSE your SELF!** You're over halfway there already.

> " Life is not a problem to be solved but a reality to be experienced."

Søren Kierkegaard

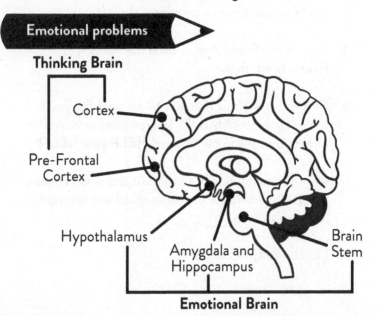

You know that looking at things differently, or reframing, helps your thinking brain (pre-frontal cortex and cortex) to manage these things by building the positive networks it needs.

What about your emotional brain, namely the brain stem and limbic system? How come when you try to look differently at something that scares you, angers you, upsets or worries you, it's a million times harder? Well, there are things your emotional brain needs a little extra help with because when it's freaking out, it can't listen to reason and logic. YET.

So, it decides 'Teenage owner, we have a problem!'

Choosing to view a problem as an opportunity to experience and overcome it, or to **TAME IT!**, is a great way of looking at your problem differently. You just need to provide your emotional brain with the right support to help it do so. Simples. Off you pop then. Shortest chapter ever!

Ah, well no. You see, your emotional brain is extremely strong-willed because it has a very important job. The most important of all important jobs. It has to keep you safe and away from danger. And ALIVE! This ancient part of your brain has been busy keeping living things alive since the Stone Age.

Our ancestors were surrounded by hungry, wild animals so they needed to be ready for anything that might be a threat to them. Their brains created feelings of anxiety, panic, fear and phobia to keep them alert and safe. Nowadays, our brains don't need to be so cautious but this ancient habit persists and gets in our way.

SNAP

Your brain loves to spot patterns everywhere. During adolescence, it can be exquisitely sensitive and over-reactive. Sometimes it spots a pattern, matches it to something it experienced and didn't like, and then it decides there's a PROBLEM! That's a pattern match – SNAP! If problems fester and you **avoid** thinking about them or facing them (such as going places or doing things you used to enjoy), they become more and more fixed because the unhelpful neural networks become stronger every time we avoid that thing. Guess what? You can grow unhelpful networks too!

Bob's job

Back in Chapter Two, I promised to properly introduce you to the whirlwind that is Bob, although you've already been acquainted your whole life. Bob is the name I give to your two amygdala and is the emotional control centre of your limbic system with specific responsibility for your emotional learning and emotional memory. With the hypothalamus, Bob  decides whether to switch incoming information from your senses (sight, hearing etc.) down to the emotional brain on a short circuit to be dealt with as an immediate threat to your safety, or up to the thinking brain on a long circuit to be dealt with logically. Together with the hippocampus, they will remember which way they sent the information, and they'll then repeat this time and time again in a similar situation. This is because the brain has identified a pattern and created a neural network. Great if Bob makes a good choice. Not so great if they jump to the threat too quickly, something your adolescent brain is even more likely to do until you're fully rewired.

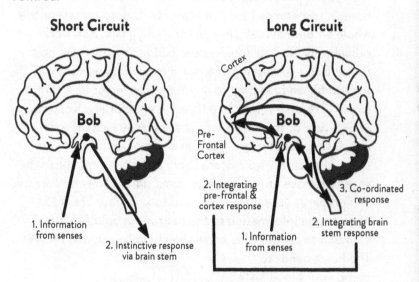

Short Circuit

Bob

1. Information from senses

2. Instinctive response via brain stem

Long Circuit

Cortex

Bob

Pre-Frontal Cortex

2. Integrating pre-frontal & cortex response

1. Information from senses

3. Co-ordinated response

2. Integrating brain stem response

Bob can misread happiness and excitement and decide these feelings are a threat to you, because happiness and excitement release the same chemicals into your bloodstream as fear. When you notice anxious feelings, always stop for a moment and take the time to check in with yourself , in case what you're feeling is actually excitement and is a lovely feeling! If it is excitement, notice it and enjoy it and this will retrain and upgrade Bob's programme.

Bob isn't actually called Bob in any science books, or anywhere else (that I know of), but they make many appearances in my books and in most of my therapy sessions with young people like yourself. And with adults. If I'm honest, sometimes I tend to promote Bob to represent the whole emotional brain, not just the amygdala. Bob works ridiculously hard so deserves the odd promotion here and there! Bob's something of a guard ~~frog~~ dog, watching out for trouble and reacting to anything that might be a threat to you. I repeat, *might be a threat* – unhelpfully, Bob's not always sure of the whole score before they kick off your instinctive response and get you all fired up through your sympathetic nervous system (SNS). The SNS organises the speedy release of two key hormones, adrenaline and cortisol, and prepares your body for action to save your life. Your nerves send information to the neurons in your heart and stomach to ensure they know they have to act, and NOW!

The heart needs to pump your blood faster and extra powerfully and your stomach needs to send its blood supply to give turbo-power to your arm and leg muscles so you can fight or run away from the threat, or the wild Stone Age beast.

We call this freeze, fight or flight.

Freeze – when your body and mind feel frozen and helpless so you're unable to do anything or escape.

Fight – when you feel angry and aggressive and your arms and legs feel powerful. You might clench your fists or stand in a confrontational way.

Flight – when you feel like you want to run away and hide, and avoid anything that feels too difficult to cope with.

The problem you've got, though, is the threat is unlikely to have been a hungry wild lion with a giant toothache that only the bones of a tasty human adolescent can cure. Even if that's how it feels. In reality, it's more likely to have been a passing thought, a look on someone's face or a bit of homework that feels too challenging. Your reaction can be out of proportion to the actual level of threat because the perceived level of threat has hijacked your emotional brain. Thanks Bob! If there really were a lion to fight or run away from, you'd automatically use up the adrenaline and cortisol pumping around your body as intended and, TADAH! Bob's job is done. Once the danger was over, your parasympathetic nervous system would switch on and regulate, or calm you down, again.

When the threat is more of the perceived kind rather than the lion kind, your body is full of the unused adrenaline and cortisol so when your vagus nerve pumps soothing chemicals to your heart, stomach, arms, legs and everywhere else to slow your breathing and make you feel more in control, it takes quite a while (at least 20 minutes and often up to an hour). This can make you feel dizzy and like your limbs are made of jelly because of the amount of chemicals it's having to make to attempt to recover you from your fear. And all that time you're still feeling in distress and maybe even in a panic. All time is not made equal (as I mentioned back in the very first paragraph of the book) and 20 minutes of panic feels so much longer than 20 minutes of doing something fun. But it will pass. It really will. Later in the chapter, you'll find lots of ways to manage and retrain Bob not to overreact so often and so much. For now, let me say that when you get the first kick of chemicals (remember what they're called?) to fire you up, you can interrupt them and take over. For example, if you're able to run on the spot, do 50 star jumps or go outside for a few minutes and look at something growing or living and then have a drink of water, you'll use them up superfast and feel better much more quickly as the vagus nerve gets to work on calming you down. Ding dong, the lion is dead! Just like that.

Black and white thinking

Bob's determined to keep you living and breathing – that's Bob's job, right? They truly believe they know best and so they send messages to shut down the thinking brain in whatever they decide is a crisis. This action prevents the thinking brain from making an 'unsafe' decision that the emotional brain might disagree with. Bob simply takes over and goes into lockdown. They can only ever make black and white decisions – stay and fight, or leg it off over the hills and far away. After all, if you were to use your thinking brain to stop and admire the beauty of the lion, wonder at its gorgeous sparkly eyes, and gently ponder whether it's related to Simba you'd be half way down its throat before you could say 'Hakuna Matata'. Black and white decisions would seem to be the best strategy when the threat is real. But it usually isn't real and that's when Bob benefits from an upgrade.

When you find yourself thinking in a very black and white way regularly, you are probably more stressed or anxious than you realise. In which case, this chapter is going to give you some great techniques for dealing with it. Or you may have got stuck in this thinking pattern. If that's the case for you, you could find **The CHOOSE YOU! Process** extremely helpful in changing that.

Faulty pattern matches

Bob can make faulty pattern matches. These happen when Bob misunderstands a pattern they've spotted and matches it wrongly. Bob assumes there's danger or something to avoid, which can lead you to years of difficulties in that particular situation. And in any situation even vaguely resembling it. You know what assumptions do, I believe?

Assumptions make an

ASSofU&ME

Here's a story about a faulty pattern match that's got a bit of a buzz about it.

So, you might have been doing a ramble, aged 9¼, in your itchy club uniform on a beautiful but hot summer's evening, under a clear blue sky with the sun setting behind the ramshackle cow sheds, as you raced your frenemy (who had the best, longest plaits in town of which you were pretty jealous) down a steep hill. Then ran to claim your victory by grabbing hold, using quite some force, of a ginormous tree. With an even more ginormous wasps' nest on a very low swinging branch right next your bright red face. And you got stung. Quite a few times. Yes, you guessed right! It was me – and, as you can see, I remember it well! Every. Last. Detail.

> Can you explain why I remember this so well?

After that, you might have been jumpy every time you heard a wasp buzzing. Understandable, no? The sound of buzzing had become linked deep in your emotional brain to the painful experience at the time of the stings, and there's your pattern match.

What if Bob then starts to react to all other kinds of buzzing that are absolutely nothing whatsoever to do with wasps, such as an electric toothbrush, phones, lawnmowers and mosquitos, and makes you irritable or angry, tearful or fearful? Well, then you've got yourself a faulty pattern match right there! And definitely some anxiety, if not a full-on phobia that meant you ran out of absolutely anywhere anytime you ever heard the slightest buzz, even if that involved embarrassing yourself in front of hundreds of people. And took you a really long time to get over because nobody told you any of this neuroscience stuff so you didn't know how to deal with it – yet. But enough about me. That was a long time ago and now I know all this stuff so it's OK! That's why I'm here to make sure you can **HELP your SELF!**

Excuse me a second, while I nip off to feed my cute pets Bazzy, Bizzy, Buzzy, Bezzy and Bozo...

Lions and hamsters
Sometimes Bob tricks you into believing something is a terrifying, fierce lion when really it's just a friendly hamster. Both animals have teeth, fur, claws, tails and shiny eyes but one is cute and no threat to you, the other is much more scary. It's easy to mistake the hamster for a lion when Bob is in charge and blocks the thinking brain from joining the party. Bob just doesn't have the brain power to make sophisticated, complex decisions by itself. Upgrading Bob to work as a team with your thinking brain is *your* job. Luckily you've got this book to show you how!

You may have had the experience of needing to remember facts or some other learning, maybe for a test or exam, but find you have gone blank and nothing is in your brain just when you really need it to be there. It's like someone flushed it out of you and it's gone forever (it hasn't, but it can truly feel like it). That happens because Bob sees your need to remember the facts as a threat – maybe that comes from you already believing you'll forget them and mess up. You're creating those negative neural networks and your supersensitive Bob responds by switching the information down to the emotional brain rather than up to the thinking brain. So, Bob reacts to the lion they imagine is prowling (the threat of messing up), rather than the hamster (the facts, that you know you know). Bob shuts down your thinking brain, and that's why you can't pull out the information you have successfully stored in there. You will, however, have enough adrenaline to run for your life – sadly, that's not much use to you in an exam room!

Write four things that get you worked up or anxious. These things probably feel like lions when you're confronted by them in your everyday life. Take a few deep breaths, clear your head and decide if each of these is really a lion or if it's actually a hamster dressed up as a lion to worry Bob. Tick the relevant box.

Problem	Lion	Hamster

Keep reading to learn ways to upgrade Bob – you'll be doing them a favour because it's exhausting to be permanently on full alert and Bob's exhaustion is your exhaustion. Bob would love to lie down on a sunny front door step and have a lazy chilled-out snooze like any other dog – but they can't because Bob is a guard dog and has to single-handedly protect you from the highly dangerous facts you had to learn for your life-threatening test or exam. But seriously, an exhausted Bob can lead to mental health problems and a lot of difficulty with everyday activities like making decisions, organising yourself and handling the usual life problems that pop up. Don't Panic! You're in good hands because this chapter is going to help you retrain Bob and get back on track.

> *"I hear and I forget.*
> *I see and I remember.*
> *I do and I understand."*
>
> **Confucius**

There may be times when your adults become frustrated with you because of the worries or stresses you are reacting to. They may not understand how bad you're feeling. It would be a good idea to sit down with them and share the parts of this book that put into words what you are going through. Remind them – they went through it once too. However long ago, every adult in your life was a teenager once.

If you've ever been really angry or scared, you'll know that when people say something like, 'There's nothing to be upset about, it's just a wasp' (or whatever it is you're upset about), the logic of what they are saying doesn't make you feel any less angry or scared. In fact, this very often makes you feel even more out of control because you feel like no one understands you or the situation. When it's an adult saying this it can really make you wobble because your emotional brain has learnt that adults can often make things OK but they have to know there's a problem they need to make OK don't they and if they can't even see there's a problem then they won't know they have to make it OK and that's not OK, OK? Aaaaaagggh!

And breathe...

I promised you some techniques to get you relaxing so you can **HELP your SELF!** so it's a great time for me to show you an excellent breathing technique that works wonders on your emotional brain, and helps bring the thinking brain back into the picture. When you can think straight, the emotional brain has less influence and you can get back in control. The rest of the tips and techniques are in this chapter too.

3:5 Breathing

This works wherever you are and whatever you are doing. The best bit is no one even knows you're doing it so if you need to feel more in control without being noticed, give it a go. If you're by yourself, you could close your eyes while you do it.

Get comfortable in a sitting position.

Notice your body breathing in and out.

After a few breaths, start to count along with yourself, making your in-breath last for the count of three and your out-breath last for the count of five, breathing smoothly.

Got it? Great! Keep going for as long as you want to or until you feel OK again.

You can dramatically improve Bob's response if you get into the habit of practising this every day for at least 10 or 15 minutes. You'll give Bob a daily dose of calm to start the reprogramming and rewiring or upgrade I mentioned. Just like any other skill, it needs to be practised if you want it to be reliable when you need it. Once you've trained yourself in the skill, you'll be able to use it in stressful situations and get calm in a hurry. There's more information about this in a few pages.

Now you're nice and calm, let me move on to anger. Don't worry, there're more techniques straight afterwards to cool you back down again.

ᗡᗡᗡᗡᗡᗡᗡᗡᗡᗡᗡᗡᗡᗡᗡᗡᗡᗡᗡᗡᗡ

Anger usually stems from an unmet emotional need in that moment, very often one that comes out of a fear. Perhaps fear that you're being unfairly attacked, criticised or judged and you feel powerless to defend yourself. Or fear that you're not respected or trusted. All your behaviour is a communication to yourself and others. When you can understand your anger and control it healthily, you'll communicate better!

ᗡᗡᗡᗡᗡᗡᗡᗡᗡᗡᗡᗡᗡᗡᗡᗡᗡᗡᗡᗡᗡ

DANGER

Have you ever noticed that **anger** is the last part of the word **danger**?

Anger is a response to feelings of danger and it also can make you appear to others as a danger.

Anger is a normal and healthy response to things that are confusing, embarrassing or unfair. Everyone feels angry at times and often, anger is a response to feeling worried or afraid of something or someone. It makes you feel overwhelmed and powerless. Although it's a natural emotion, it's a very unpleasant feeling. What you do with your angry feelings is always your responsibility.

When things or people annoy you, you can quickly become upset, angry and unreasonable. You could find you regret your words or actions after you've started to calm down. Repeated episodes of lashing out, shouting, destroying or breaking things, and insulting or hurting others can damage important relationships, make people wary of you and cause anxiety in others. It is important to work hard to control your actions when you are angry so that they pass without causing you a bigger problem.

Without healthy ways to manage your anger, you might turn it on yourself and develop mental health conditions that are self-damaging.

☐☐☐☐☐☐☐☐☐☐☐☐☐☐☐☐☐☐☐☐☐☐☐☐

Humans become functionally stupid when angry. You won't always be able to use your usual logic and intelligence because of Bob! You'll be drowning in brain chemicals that hide your rational thoughts so you can survive the moment – this was really important for humans in the Stone Age, but as we don't have the same threats now, we have to upgrade and rewire Bob's response to suit our modern world.

☐☐☐☐☐☐☐☐☐☐☐☐☐☐☐☐☐☐☐☐☐☐☐☐

Early warning signs of anger
Everyone is different but anger tends to create similar warning signs in most people. Look out for your heart beating harder and faster in your chest. Your tummy might twinge, you might clench your mouth, face and fists, your whole body might feel tense and out of control and you might have thought about hurting people and destroying things. Bob is in full-on FIGHT mode.

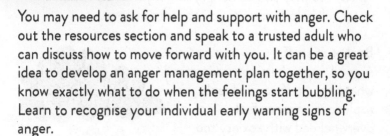

Getting help

You may need to ask for help and support with anger. Check out the resources section and speak to a trusted adult who can discuss how to move forward with you. It can be a great idea to develop an anger management plan together, so you know exactly what to do when the feelings start bubbling. Learn to recognise your individual early warning signs of anger.

An anger management plan might look like this:

1. List your warning signs – e.g. hot hands, feeling out of control...

2. Walk away and find somewhere to sit until you're calmer or do something energetic to use the adrenaline and cortisol up.

3. Think about something happy or count to 10 – or 100!

4. Breathe deliberately – in for three and out for five, keep going until Bob has stood down.

5. Have a drink of water – this fast-tracks Bob into a normal pattern.

6. Get help if you need it.

It's possible that your anger might explode and take you by surprise from time to time. When this happens, your stress levels may have crept up without you realising. If you notice this becoming more common for you, build in some of the relaxation activities to your daily routine to reduce your stress. You may also be hungry or dehydrated. A drink of water will help to restore you to more balance.

Bucket of stuff

A good way to help you understand what happens if you suddenly explode in anger or feel overwhelmed with anxiety too quickly is to think of yourself as a bucket, full to the brim. When it rains, which it will, it's not going to take much to make it overflow and spill out all over the place, spoiling your day. If you're able to regularly empty your bucket in a predictable and measured way by doing relaxation activities, you'll have a lot more space to think and control your feelings and it will take a lot more rain to get you anywhere near overflowing. And that's got to be better for everyone, especially you. Amphibians, not so much.

Get busy, resting!
Your brain needs time when you are resting and relaxing and doing nothing in particular, like daydreaming, doodling, walking or exercising in nature, listening to music, looking at art or reading your favourite comics, magazines and books. Chill time is just as important as all the other things you need to do.

Relaxation is vital to keep your body, brain and mind healthy. It can take practice to be able to relax. If you've been very anxious or stressed, it may feel a bit strange to start relaxing but keep trying and you will soon start to feel better, more focused, more confident and more in control.

Your brain needs regular hydration. Drink a few glasses of water throughout the day and any time you feel stressed so the anxiety-busting chemical these techniques create have an easier journey and get to work quickly.

Techniques and tips – time to pick'n'mix!

I've been promising this section of the book for quite a while now and we are finally here! This menu offers really effective ways for you to elbow worry out of the way and feel chilled and calm. Some are techniques and some are tips, but they are all based on neuroscience. Master these and you'll find it easier to cope when Bob kicks off. Bob is your Stone Age warrior. You can conquer Bob with your inner thinking brain warrior and take control.

Find a private place where you feel confident to explore the suggestions and remember, your invisible audience isn't real. No one can see you and no one would judge you for trying to be happier and more confident! Try the techniques and activities that seem to make the most sense to you first. Then try the others! Find your favourites and put them into practice, regularly. If you haven't already got one, you might want to find a notebook or journal to use alongside the techniques. Or why not use sticky notes to record the ideas that help you the most and put them in places that'll be useful when you really need them. Go on, grow your neural networks!

Don't forget about the **3:5 breathing** that we did just before the section on anger. Make it your go-to technique and practise it every day. Breathing mindfully in this way resets your brain like the 'turn off and on again' trick you use with electronic devices. It also retrains Bob to team up with your thinking brain and brings their programming up to date.

Bad feelings will pass.
They're just traffic in your mind and body.
Don't let them park in your brain!

Remember, it's not you, it's your Bob!
Give Bob time and they will adjust and
get you back on track.

"He who conquers himself is the mightiest warrior."

Confucius

I've put together this menu for you with excellent techniques and tips for you to try and choose your favourite. We are all individual and so are our preferences. Use the exercises that work for you and you enjoy doing. You can disregard any you don't enjoy.

Let's kick off with some alternative breathing techniques that I use in therapy work with my teenage patients. Like any new skill, breathing techniques need regular practice – about 15 minutes every day should make a real difference. Once you've got the hang of them, you'll be able to use them in any upsetting or stressful situation to stay in control. Bob will often give you loads of excuses why you shouldn't stick with breathing techniques and will try to distract you or make you find it uncomfortable at first – remember, Bob truly thinks these situations are dangerous because of their Stone Age programme so it stands to reason they won't want you to be 'tricked' into calming down. Take control of Bob for their own good (and, more importantly, for yours!) by using these retraining techniques to upgrade the programme into one that's suitable for the modern world where you aren't dodging lions lurking behind every tree.

Breathe, Be, Believe
Do this breathing exercise anywhere and anytime. It's perfect for growing your neural networks. Sit or stand with a straight back and your arms relaxed.

- **BREATHE**
  Breathe in. Focus on drawing the air into your belly.
  Picture yourself being filled with calming air and
  breathe in slowly saying 'BREATHE' in your head.

- **BE**
  Picture yourself looking calm, hold your breath for
  a second or two saying 'BE' in your head.

- **BELIEVE**
  Picture yourself feeling really calm and believing
  positive things about yourself, breathe out slowly
  as though you're a softly deflating balloon saying
  'BELIEVE' in your head.

Keep going until you're back in control

Exchange it up
You can change how you're feeling – deliberately – by
breathing and thinking differently about your experiences.
Try this thought exchange breathing exercise:

Sit or stand comfortably. Picture yourself feeling fine and
stress-free. You could think of a time when that's how you
felt, or use your imagination.

Breathe in slowly and deeply and say in your mind,
'I'm breathing in calm'.

Hold your breath for a second or two and say in your mind,
'I can sit with these feelings'.

Breathe out slowly and gently and say in your mind,
'I'm breathing out stress/anger/ upset'.

Repeat this six times. Then drink water.

Triangle breathing
Triangle breathing is a great way to calm your whole brain and put you back in control. Run your finger along the first side of a triangle as you breathe in, then run it along the second side as you hold your breath and smile, and finally run it along the third side as you slowly breathe out.

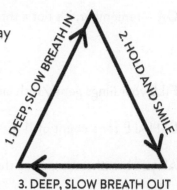

1. DEEP, SLOW BREATH IN

2. HOLD AND SMILE

3. DEEP, SLOW BREATH OUT

Experiment with different finger running speeds to find the best method for you. You can use the palm of your hand if you don't have any pen and paper.

NO FEAR

NOTICE the warning signs in your body

OK – remember, it's not a threat

FILL your lungs gently with air for a count of seven

EXHALE for a count of 11

AS you breathe out, notice three things you can **see**

RELAX

NOTICE the warning signs in your body

OK – remember, it's not a threat

FILL your lungs gently with air for a count of seven

EXHALE for a count of 11

AS you breathe out, notice three things you can **hear**

RELAX

NOTICE the warning signs in your body

OK – remember, it's not a threat

FILL your lungs gently with air for a count of seven

EXHALE for a count of 11

AS you breathe out, notice three things you can **feel**

RELAX

Finger Breathing
This is a really 'handy' skill you can have at your fingertips
wherever you go. Spread your hand out on your knee or a
table. If you prefer, you can draw around your hand and use

the picture. Notice your body breathing in and out. Take your pointer finger from the opposite hand, put it on the bottom knuckle of your thumb. Slowly trace up to the tip, breathing in as you do. Stop at the top, hold your breath for a second, then trace back down the other side while you breathe out. Keep going until you've traced every finger in the same way, smoothly. Remember to keep your breathing smooth too. Repeat this six times, and make sure all your attention is on your hand and your breath.

Now you've explored the different breathing exercises, you're ready to move to the next level of the menu.

All in the detail

In a notebook or on some spare paper, draw or write about a situation or something that gets you feeling afraid or panicky even though it's not dangerous. Add lots of detail. Take your time to really notice every part of it and draw or describe it carefully. You can stop to do any of the breathing techniques listed, or another that you like, as often as you need to if you feel a bit uncomfortable while you're doing this. We know that facing our feelings this way really helps Bob to see straight and stops their assumption that the situation is a danger to you. Keep going until your whole mind feels peaceful looking at the picture or re-reading what you've written. Now add new words or phrases to your picture or writing to remind yourself that it can't hurt you here – perhaps around the edges, over the top, underneath or however you want. Put that old fear in its place and tell it you're no longer afraid – you're a **warrior**.

Identify

This technique will help you notice your own behaviour patterns which will give you more of a sense of control.

It's best to do it in writing but you could just think them through. Read the instructions before you start so you can decide how to lay the information out.

Step one
List the kind of situations you find stressful in any order. Next to each one, describe how you usually react to it. What do you notice? If it's not immediately obvious, keep an ongoing list and look for patterns in your reactions.

Step two
Now describe how you would prefer to react to each situation, and/or in general. Maybe you could use a different colour pen for each section?

Remember what Socrates said: 'Know Yourself!' If you know how you might react, you can change your actions and prevent the problem from bothering you.

Recognise your early warning signs
Next time you're anxious, stressed or angry, use this list to help you recognise your early warning signs and as soon as you realise what's happening, practise your calming techniques. Then record the signs you noticed and keep reminding yourself of your warning signs anytime you need to. The more you control Bob, the quicker they get upgraded and reprogrammed and the sooner you can leave your stress behind you.

Feeling separate from everyone else	Hot or cold face and/or hands
Feeling dizzy, faint or light headed	Fast breathing
Hard to swallow	Tight chest
Racing or fluttery heart	Numb or tingly hands
Sweaty palms	Hot or cold waves

Feeling sick   Upset stomach butterflies
Trembling or shaking   Numb or tingly feet
Something else?

Safe place visualisation
Find a calm, quiet spot where you can relax. Breathe in and
out deeply for three minutes. In time with your in-breath,
say in your head 'breathe in calm' and in time with your out-
breath, say 'breathe out stress'.

Now, imagine a place where you could feel totally safe and
comfortable, maybe somewhere you've seen, been to, heard
about, read about or dreamed about. It's a special safe place
where everything feels peaceful, calm and secure. Spend 10
to 15 minutes observing all the things you love in this safe
place.

Powerful Hands
Pick a quiet, calm spot and lie down. Close your eyes and
picture yourself in a place that feels familiar, comfortable
and safe. Breathe deeply and slowly. Now, focus all your
attention on your hands and imagine you are warming them
up. Notice your hands start to actually feel warmer. When
you've mastered this skill, try spreading the warm feeling
up your arms and down into your stomach. Can you do
the same with your feet and legs? Keep going and you'll be
feeling calm and confident in no time.

Sing something silly
Make up a silly song or sing your favourite song in the silliest
voice you can make – it will remind your brain to have a
giggle as well as calm down. Maybe you could try to double-
speed a rap or make it really slow.

SSS
Cut out sugar, focus on your strengths and get some sleep!

We know that sugar is fuel for Bob and they're way more jumpy with poor sleep. Your whole body will feel healthier if you master this tip. Remember that your strengths are what you can build on so keep them uppermost in your mind. Being aware of your strengths changes how you feel, think and see yourself as well as what you believe about yourself.

Heart healer
We all feel heavy-hearted at times. It's important to remember that you're part of a bigger world which is incredible and awesome – just like you. Slowing down your heart-rate is really good for your brain-body. You can get a friend to join you with this if you feel self-conscious doing it by yourself.

Go outside and find something natural that's living, moving or growing. This could be anything, like a flower, insect, clouds or the moon. Start off by checking your pulse and notice how fast it's going. Now focus on watching the natural thing for a couple of minutes. Don't do anything except notice the thing you are looking at. Look at it as if you are seeing it for the first time ever. Then find three more things to look at and repeat the activity. Check your pulse again right at the end and see if you've slowed it down. What do you notice about the way you're feeling?

Talk 12
Talk to someone for 12 minutes about anything you like. It doesn't have to be about something you're worried about, or feeling negative about – but it can be if you like. Hobbies, sports, fashion, animals, comics, books, music and film all make for good conversations.

Thank U, next!

This technique is amazing for getting you relaxed and calm before an important event and it's even better for helping you get to sleep if you do it in bed.

1. Find a quiet place where you can spend at least 15 minutes relaxing without interruption.

2. Sit or lie down and get comfortable. Uncross your arms and legs to let your circulation flow freely.

3. Take a few slow, deep breaths into your belly, using any of the breathing techniques you enjoy. Let your belly expand as you breathe in and pull in or contract as you breathe out.

4. Tense up your face by squinting as tightly as possible. Use your face muscles to pull your cheeks to your eyes. Clench your teeth. Hold this as you breathe in for a count of five and say **THANK U** in your mind for all the things your face does for you.

5. Breathe out slowly for a count of eight and gently release all the tension in your face, as if a magnet is drawing it all out of you.

6. Repeat this twice more or until your relaxed face feels light and refreshed. Take your time and relax before you move on.

7. Move your focus to your neck and shoulders and repeat the process on them by tensing them up and holding as you breathe in for a count of five. Remember to say **THANK U** in your mind as you

breathe out. Repeat as needed and relax again.

8. Keep moving through the muscle groups in your body, **one at a time**, repeating the whole method outlined above with your arms (one at a time if you prefer), hands (make a fist), chest, abdomen, buttocks, legs (one at a time if you prefer) tensing your thighs, knees, calves and finally your feet. Again, remember to say **THANK U** in your mind every time you breathe out for each muscle group.

9. Spend some time enjoying how relaxed you feel. Say **THANK U** in your mind to your whole brilliant and awesome body as you breathe out. You can stop at this point if you want to.

10. If you'd like to, you can repeat the whole process or work back up the body to your face and neck.

Body Scan

Become your very own scanning machine and notice yourself chilling out. You can download Body Scan exercises or mindfulness meditations from apps and the internet (see the resources section for suggestions).

1. Get yourself comfortable somewhere calm and decide to relax. You can stand, sit or lie down. It's particularly helpful to do the body scan lying down if you are using it to help you get to sleep.

2. Take a few slow, deep breaths into your belly, using any of the breathing techniques you enjoy. Let your belly expand as you breathe in and pull in or contract as you breathe out.

3. Notice your feet. Slowly bring all your attention down to them. Begin observing and being curious about any sensations as you scan those feet, but don't try to explain them. Keep breathing deeply as you release any tension from the feet.

4. Scan your whole body concentrating on one body area at a time – your lower legs, thighs, abdomen, chest, hands, arms, shoulders, neck, face and head.

5. Now go back to your feet and this time gently scan your whole body from the tips of your toes to the top of your head. Notice where you feel tightness, pain or pressure. Decide to release those sensations.

6. Rest for a few moments and bring your breathing back to normal.

Yoga

The beliefs that grow are the ones you feed. Let's feed your strong, inner warrior in your thinking brain! Try this by yourself or with a friend to read out the instructions.
There are lots of excellent yoga tutorials online you could explore, too.

Warrior 1 pose – **I AM STRONG**

Stand straight, feet together, arms out at the sides.

Step forward, bend your front knee, back leg straight behind you.

Arch your back, stretch arms and

hands up to the sky.

Look straight ahead with a powerful expression on your face.

Take a deep breath for a count of three.

As you breathe out, say aloud 'I AM STRONG'.

Let all the breath go.

Stay in the pose and do this four more times.

Breathe normally, bring arms down to sides and feet back together with straight legs.

Swap legs and repeat.

Warrior 2 pose – **I AM POWERFUL**

From Warrior 1, stretch arms out in front of you.

Turn your chest, bring one arm out to the front, the other stretched behind you.

Look straight ahead with a powerful expression on your face.

Take a deep breath for a count of three.

As you breathe out, say aloud 'I AM POWERFUL'.

Let all the breath go.

Stay in the pose and do this four more times.

Breathe normally, turn your chest the other way and glide arms around so they swap positions and repeat.

Warrior 3 – **I AM IMPORTANT**

From Warrior 2, bring both arms in front of you.

Straighten your front leg and lift your back foot off the ground a little.

Open arms wider for balance if needed.

Look straight ahead with a powerful expression on your face.

Take a deep breath for a count of three.

As you breathe out, say aloud '**I AM IMPORTANT**'.

Let all the breath go.

Stay in the pose and do this four more times.

Breathe normally, bring arms down to sides, feet back together with straight legs. Swap legs and repeat.

Peaceful pebbles

Find some garden pebbles or buy them in a garden centre. Wash, dry and paint them or use permanent markers, or leave them natural. Write inspiring, comforting words and phrases on them and keep them on your desk or carry them around with you to remind you how to calm down. You can feel them and look at them to occupy your senses in a crisis.

Calm box

Fiddle your way out of anxiety and create a calm box! Find a box that you can re-use or you could buy a small container that you like . Decorate it if you wish. Fill it with items you like the feel of and then you can fiddle with them whenever you need to relax or calm down. Here are some ideas but you'll know what works for you:

Small cuddly toys, modelling clay, fabric with scent sprayed on, hand lotion, stress ball, fidget toys, figures, rubber bands, bubble wrap, peaceful pebbles, beads.

Memory Jar

Find an empty jar with a lid. Decorate it with pens or stickers. Make a label for it. Keep it somewhere you can see it every day. Every time you have a lovely memory or get a compliment, do something really well or feel powerful, just write it down on a slip of paper or a sticky note, fold it up and put it safely in the jar.

Whenever you need to, just grab your jar and read all the messages until you feel calm. This is a great bedtime routine to help you end your day on a positive note.

Dance

Yep, that's it. Just dance. For as long as you like, to whatever you like, wherever you like and with whoever you like.

Hug a pug

Well, any dog, amphibian or human will do – just ask permission! A hug is a wonderful way to get you feeling calm thanks to the *oxytocin* it releases, counteracting the adrenaline and cortisol of stress, anxiety, anger and fear.

Ask someone you trust for a hug right now. If you can't hug someone you'd like to, close your eyes and imagine the hug. Notice how it feels in your stomach, chest and mind. Bob can't tell the difference between a real or imagined hug, but they – and you - can feel the benefit, either way.

Describe your tribe

When people make you feel great, you should spend as much time as you can with them – they are your sunshine people. Draw your tribe and include whoever makes you feel great! Write their name under their picture and add a positive comment about each one. If you don't enjoy drawing, why not make a paper collage from photos? Alternatively, use an editing programme to create your tribe and perhaps print it out as stickers or a picture you can frame?

Mindful moments

Try this experiment to really notice what happens when you eat. You might prefer to do it with a friend or your adults. You can use a piece of chocolate if you don't like raisins. Make sure you don't use anything you're allergic to.

You will need: one raisin for you and one for a friend you choose to do this with.

Sit comfortably and take two or three comfortable deep breaths.

Place the raisin in your hand.

Look closely at the raisin with your full attention as though you've never seen one before. Examine the wrinkles closely.

Now close your eyes. Place the raisin on one of your fingers and gently move it around on your hand, exploring it carefully. What does the raisin feel like?

Hold the raisin near your nose and notice its smell. Does anything interesting happen in your mouth or stomach?

Slowly bring the raisin up to your mouth then rub it across your lips and notice what that feels like. It might feel difficult not to just pop it in your mouth!

Put the raisin on your tongue and let it sit there for a few seconds. Don't chew it. Just leave it on your tongue and notice how it feels.

Now very slowly begin to chew it. Bite it gently and notice what it feels like between your teeth.

Try not to swallow it just yet. Wait until the taste fills your mouth, then swallow it down.

Notice your breathing again and then open your eyes.

Exam stress technique

And finally, because your teen years are likely to be peppered with the odd test or exam here and there...

As we've already seen earlier in this chapter, exams can make you stressed. Here are some tips to keep you relaxed and positive.

- Breathe slowly and remind yourself that you're doing your best. You are stronger and smarter than your anxiety or stress.

- Revise little and often, for no more than 45 minutes in one block. Take regular breaks, eat healthy snacks and drink water. Go outside for 15 minutes if you can between revision blocks.

- Picture yourself walking into the exam calmly, turning over the paper with a smile and writing down what you know. Believe in yourself – you've got this!

- No one's whole future depends on an exam result. They're important but they're not a one-time thing. You can often re-sit exams if you need to.

You could look up exam tips online if you want more detailed advice on how to manage the practical stuff around revision and preparing for exams.

Hopefully, somewhere in that pick'n'mix menu, you'll have found ways to **HELP your SELF!** that work for you in your everyday life. Even if you're not aware of feeling stressed or overwhelmed, it's a good idea to build some of the techniques into your regular self-care routines. That way, you'll have a valve to slowly release any tension, which is way healthier than bottling it up.

Let it out

A fun strategy that works a treat as a tension valve is spending time with friends you trust and having a properly good laugh. My amazing writer friend, Sarah, is what I like to call a sunshine person. She always seems to know when I need a chuckle and spending time with her feels like floating on a cloud on the sunniest day, or my football team winning the league and the sky raining chocolate drops. Do you have a Sunshine Sarah in your life? I waited a long time for mine, so if you haven't found yours yet, be patient! Of course, your sunshine person might not be called Sarah! They have all sorts of different names. Sunshine Sarahs also come in all forms – from a beloved pet, to a grandparent to... well, anyone really!

Write the name or names of your Sunshine Sarah or Sarahs here – or draw them if you prefer. Or you could do both.

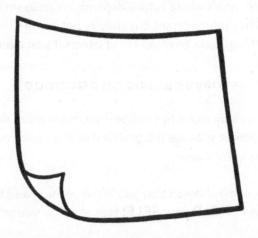

We all have mental health and physical health and each one can experience a minor disturbance like a brief period of anxiety (perhaps around exams) or a sore throat. Your brain is an organ like any other part of your body and it reacts and responds to the threats it sees and feels, including disease and injury, and the overall health of your way of life. An illness, mental or physical, is more serious and needs the right attention.

There are times in all our lives when, despite our best efforts, the pressure of everything we have to cope with is too great and things can go a bit off course for a while. It's happened to me and maybe it's happened to you before, too? Imagine filling a super strong balloon with air and when it's massive and feels really stretched, fragile and full up, you just keep going and going piling more and more into it. It can be hard to recognise when you're getting too full up especially if this happens slowly over a long time but it can have quite an impact when we ignore or can't see the signs. Eventually something will give, and you'll be forced to deal with whatever's been getting to you.

Mental health disorders

Everyone worries or feels nervous or stressed some of the time. That's normal and to be expected. If anxiety or panic start to interfere too often, or you are unable to shake off negative or painful feelings, it is possible something more is going on.

TRIGGER WARNING

At your age, you are more likely to develop a mental health disorder but that doesn't mean you'll definitely develop one or that, if you do, you'll always have it. If things start to feel out of balance, you're upset all the time or you struggle to know what is real and what isn't, your mental health may need some treatment. People recover and treatments really do work. If you get help, you can recover.

> # "The wound is the place where the light enters you."
>
> ## Rumi

There are many forms of mental disorders and some of the main ones are detailed here. Use this list to help you explain to a trusted adult what you're experiencing. Plus, in the resources section, there are lots of websites with great information for you to find out more:

Anxiety disorder
When you get worried about one or more things and the worry gets in the way of your life and causes you to avoid things on a regular basis.

Panic disorder
When you feel like you can't cope and are overwhelmed by fear so you can't think rationally for periods of time.

Phobia
When something causes you to experience extreme fear that feels life-threatening. Can cause panic and make you behave irrationally and sometimes dangerously to avoid the situation.

PTSD (Post-Traumatic Stress Disorder)
When you have a deeply frightening or upsetting experience and it doesn't fade with time. It feels like it's still happening when you remember it.

Depression
When you feel down for more than a couple of weeks and nothing makes you feel better. You can find it difficult to find any energy and you may feel you can't be bothered to do anything.

Eating disorders
When eating too much or too little becomes a problem for your health. Eating problems are common and can affect anyone of any body shape, gender or lifestyle. Being anxious or stressed can trigger eating problems.

Mood disorders
When your mood changes frequently and you go from feeling too high to too low in cycles, or you feel too high for too long.

OCD (Obsessive Compulsive Disorder)
When you have distressing thoughts, see images or experience feelings and need everything to be done a certain way so you feel better or 'just right' again.

Perception disorders
When reality is different for you from how others perceive it. You might feel muddled or not know if you're dreaming or if something is really happening. You might hear, smell, see or feel things that aren't there. **Body dysmorphia** is a common perception disorder (see Chapter Six).

Self-harm

When you cause injury to your body to relieve pressure, punish yourself or feel connected.

Estimates suggest that at least 1 in 10 young people will use self-harm to manage emotional chaos and pain at some point during adolescence. You're more likely to self-harm if others around you are doing it. It is three times more common in girls but boys are increasingly more likely to hurt themselves. Self-harm can lead to life-threatening injuries and infections or accidental death. Some people who self-harm have suicidal thoughts but this is not usually true – in fact, self-harm is more likely to be a way of trying to deal with life rather than to end it.

Both emotional and physical pain occur in the same brain areas and we know that social rejection causes intense emotional pain as real as any physical pain. Self-harming when emotions peak can reduce the pain and bring about hypo-arousal resulting in a temporary numb sensation in the body and mind which may provide relief to the young person. Some young people already feel numb and disconnected and use self-harm to experience the pain it creates. Whatever the reason, self-harming is never a healthy way to manage your emotions and can create a loop that feels impossible to break.

- Rage, self-hatred, a wish to punish yourself and others, anger, sadness, guilt, shame, anxiety, depression, frustration, hopelessness, powerlessness and other negative feelings can all trigger self-harming behaviours and keep them going. It is important to get support from an experienced professional in order to work through the underlying distress and find healthy ways to regulate your feelings and break the loop. Self-harm is hurting yourself on purpose, for example by scratching, hitting, picking, hair-pulling, biting, cutting, burning, overdosing on medication or taking harmful substances, drinking alcohol or taking drugs to excess.

- Self-harming isn't usually linked to a wish to take your own life but accidental suicides can and do happen as a result. Some young people who self-harm do have suicidal thoughts and wishes.

- Self-harm is an attempt to communicate and manage your emotional turmoil and feel better. It can give you temporary relief but this doesn't last because it doesn't deal with what is really going on for you.

- Self-harm isn't a mental illness although it is an indicator of mental distress, which left untreated can lead to mental illness.

- Self-harming often happens when you feel isolated and find it too difficult to cope with or share your painful feelings with a trusted adult. Support can help you to feel less alone and reduce or stop your harming.

- Sometimes people experiencing relationship difficulties use self-harm to cope. It is important to seek help with this to prevent you becoming more isolated.

- You may need to attend A&E after harming yourself. Wounds need proper care to prevent serious infection. Hospital staff see all kinds of self-harm and may be able to suggest where you can get support as well as take care of your physical health after harming.

- Doctors can refer you for support or you could look for a therapist with experience in supporting young people who harm. School staff can be helpful but they can't be expected to manage all your emotional needs and may not always be available. Ask for a safety plan to be written with you.

- Supporting someone who self-harms is upsetting and confusing. Be patient and learn about why they are self-harming without taking it personally. It is important to make clear agreements with the young person but make sure they have choices and a say in what happens next.

Suicidal thoughts and ideation
When you think about ending your life and how you could do it because you're feeling unhappy or unwell.

TRIGGER WARNING

If you're experiencing any of these upsetting problems, get help. Do it today. It's not your fault and it doesn't mean you're weak. It takes huge strength to face your problems and ask for help. You are precious and deserve to be supported. Speak to a trusted adult if you need help finding the right support. Check out the resources section for more advice and guidance for you and your adults, if you choose to share it with them. Adults don't always have the answers so they may need to know where to start – you can help them with that!

"The world breaks everyone and afterwards many are strong at the broken places."

Ernest Hemingway

In Japan, the ancient art of Kintsugi (金継ぎ,) is used to mend broken pottery, using sap from trees and gold or silver powder. Pots that were once broken are considered unique and even more beautiful, for having been broken.

Mind bones

Sometimes you need time to heal a broken bone, to recover from a cold, to get over a tummy bug or other infection. Why should your brain be any different? Are you ashamed of a broken arm? Nope, you get a neon cast and make all your friends write silly/rude/dodgy/embarrassing (delete as appropriate) messages ALL OVER IT! You wave it about and get a ton of sympathy and make people laugh with your hilarious tales of how it happened, what it's like to eat spaghetti with it and how interesting it makes going to the loo.

Why should your brain be any different to your arm? Why do we feel ashamed when our brain does what any other part of us is allowed to do? Maybe you feel you should be able to keep it healthy in spite of everything going on for you? Maybe because when you're young, your well-meaning adults will often try to distract you from feeling upset and tell you you're OK even when you don't feel OK. They're trying to be kind but it can be confusing to your emotional brain if you never learn to process the feeling and are discouraged from spending time and energy thinking about it. This can also create the added idea that you *should* be OK because you're being told you are.

THERE. ARE. NO. SHOULDS.

We don't say 'your arm shouldn't have broken' or 'it should have been strong enough to not break when that cricket ball hit it'. Maybe, on another day, at a minutely different angle or with a different ball it would have just got a sprain and you'd only need a few cubes of ice and a bandage from the nurse or doctor and a painkiller to stop it aching. Maybe it wouldn't have broken. But it did. And no-one minds that it broke.

Unless it's a mind that broke and then people seem to mind.

Don't mind. Get help. Take the best care of yourself – you deserve it. Really mind your mind. And if it breaks a bit for a while, don't mind. Don't be ashamed. Just get help. Use this book and let it take you as far as it can. If the problem won't go away or keeps coming back, you'll need to speak to one of your adults and go to a professional like your school nurse, GP, counsellor or therapist. I'm sure you already know by now that there's a load of resources at the back of this book to help you find the right help – use them however you wish. And if you can't find the right help – email me*, I'll guide you to the best place for you.

> # "Because you are alive, everything is possible."
>
> ## Thích Nhất Hạnh

1 in 4 people across the world will have a mental health problem at some time in their lives. Treatments can be very effective. If you have a problem with anxiety or your mental health now, it doesn't mean you'll always have a problem. If you are worried about anything in this chapter, talk to someone you trust. If you fear you might hurt yourself or you're having suicidal thoughts, it's important to speak to someone urgently. There is always a way forward. Your mind can tell you that whatever you're worried about has never happened to anyone before, but helplines (there's several at the back of this book that you can contact) can listen to you compassionately without judging you. They have heard every imaginable problem, situation and circumstance and have been trained to know how to help you. You are not alone. You are loved.

*see the resources section for contact details.

Go dotty!

In this chapter, you've learnt why your brain behaves like a Stone Age warrior sometimes. You've been introduced to Bob and learnt how to bring them under control. You've seen that sometimes you may need to get help from a professional if the problem doesn't go away or keeps coming back. You are not alone if this happens to you.

Add any new dots you've uncovered here and keep working on joining them up to understand yourself as you read through the book. Add more dots if you need to.

- E.g. I don't always look after myself well or give myself time to relax and laugh.

- _____

- _____

- _____

Get connected!

Connect these dots – are you retraining your thinking brain to conquer this section, yet? You'll see what it is in the end...

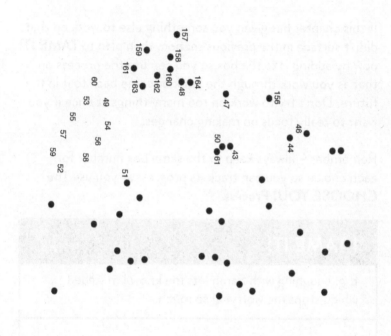

The CHOOSE YOU! Process

TAME IT!

It's time to **TAME IT!** Write down what you can do to **HELP your SELF!** with the things you named, claimed and reframed in the boxes in the previous chapters.

If this chapter has given you something else to work on that didn't surface in the previous section, then plan to **TAME IT!** now by adding it to the box so you can use the process on that as you work through the book or come back to it in the future. Don't try to work on too many things at once if you want to really focus on making changes.

Remember – always keep to the same box number for each choice so you can track its progress as you use **The CHOOSE YOU! Process**

I TAME IT!
E.g. Laughing with Sarah lets me know I'm valued which stops me worrying so much.
1
2
3
4
5

Keep reading and find out in Chapter Six how to **LOVE your SELF!** and start to **RECLAIM IT!**

CHAPTER SIX

RECLAIM IT!

LOVE YOUR SELF!

This chapter will:

1. Focus on the **RECLAIM IT!** section of **The CHOOSE YOU! Process**

2. Work out what things stop you from treating yourself in a loving way and feeling good about yourself

3. Introduce you to ways you can **LOVE your SELF!**, show you why it matters and help you identify if you need to show yourself more love

4. Encourage you to expect to be treated with respect, understand healthy and unhealthy relationships and know when to walk away

5. Explain how to practise self-care and how some risky behaviours might cause problems for your mind or body

6. Help you to think positively about your own body image and learn how to feel good about your incredible, one-of-a-kind brain-body

7. Lead on to Chapter Seven

> ## "Love is the bridge between you and everything."
>
> ### Rumi

LOVE your SELF!

What does that mean? Am I encouraging you to expect everyone to be blown away by how amazing you are every single day, suggesting you post 900 selfies in one evening with the comment, 'Don't you think I look phenomenal?', or message all your mates to say you're the next big thing about to hit 'X-Factor' and you're guaranteed to win? Well, no. I'm not suggesting that you should be self-obsessed! A splash of modesty and self-awareness is a jolly good thing, and it's always important to consider how other people feel around you. What I am encouraging you to do is see your good points and feel you are a valued and valuable person.

Most of us can't feel fantastic about ourselves all the time but we can all still love ourselves. By which I mean treat yourself kindly, as you would a very close friend who you value and care about and who is going to be around for the longest time; take good care of your physical and mental health by doing the things your brain-body needs from you; and show yourself respect and expect the same from others in your life. The way you treat yourself is a very good indicator to others about how they should treat you.

> *"If you look for perfection,
> you'll never be content."*

Leo Tolstoy

Perfectly imperfect

YOU ARE NOT PERFECT

You never will be perfect. Perfect doesn't exist in the real world, only in your imagination about other people or yourself.

Striving to achieve and present a perfect version of you to the world and to yourself is very unhealthy and, I hate to say, is always going to end in a massive disappointment. Not because there's anything wrong with YOU but because the closer you get to your idea of perfection, the further away you'll inevitably put your next goalpost. By all means, strive to be the best you can be, but you'll never find out what that is by constantly criticising or finding fault with yourself. The most effective way to discover it is to spend time on yourself and with yourself. Just as you've been doing in this book, identify what your needs are and put your efforts into that. This chapter is all about how to reclaim the issues you've been working on after learning how to tame the things you identified at the beginning of **The CHOOSE YOU! Process.** What that means is you proudly embracing and shouting from the rooftops that this imperfection is a part of you.

In ancient Persia, tribe members wove carpets in fine detail to reflect their group's stories. It would take them years and many of the tribe would be involved. They knew they were imperfect, as we all are, so they would intentionally create flaws or mistakes in the carpet, which led to the old proverb: *Perfectly imperfect and precisely imprecise.*

Since the 16th century, Japanese potters created beautiful, irregular pots to illustrate the wabi-sabi aesthetic, which sees beauty in the imperfect and the incomplete.

I AM NOT PERFECT but I'm good enough!

> "When you are content to be simply yourself and don't compare or compete, everyone will respect you."
>
> Lao Tzu

✗ Don't compare!

It's human nature to want to see how you fit in with others. As you know, your teen brain is programmed to notice everyone around you and keep you very aware of yourself in different social situations and when you are by yourself. Troubles come when you start to judge yourself against what others are doing, how they look, what they're wearing and who they're hanging out with. It's possible to do this so much that you start to lose sight of what is unique about you and what it is that others see in you. You might stop listening to the positive things your adults tell you, or why your friends enjoy your company. In short, you fall into the trap of comparing yourself to others and that NEVER ENDS WELL! Want to know why?

The problem is, there will always be someone smarter than you, not as smart as you, shorter than you, taller than you, thinner than you, fatter than you, not as good looking as you, better looking than you and this list could go on for the rest of the book. And then into *Book Two – The Wasted Years*.

Where does that leave you if all you're doing is seeing how you compare instead of noticing what there is to be celebrated about you? Not one of the people you compare yourself to is perfect either. You are identifying different things in different people to measure yourself against. You're literally creating a metaphorical monster – a total mishmash of everyone's best bits – to taunt, torment and torture yourself with.

Let's take a look at you.

Tell me three things other people, friends or adults like about you and three different things you like about you on these sticky notes. You decide what those things are.

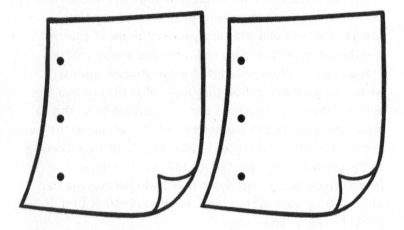

Right to be wrong

You are allowed to make mistakes and mess up. You are learning about yourself and the world every single day. It's a complicated world with so many things that can happen in just one day (or one hour, frankly!). You will keep making mistakes your whole life and if you focus on the positives, you'll learn from them too. Welcome to the human race.

Mistakes have led to some of the most significant inventions – like fire, medicines, plastic and microwave ovens! Maybe you know something you can do now because you made mistakes?

> "We ourselves feel that what we are doing is just a drop in the ocean. But the ocean would be less because of that missing drop."
>
> Mother Teresa

Good enough

At school and at home, your adults will be showing you and telling you how to be better and do better. At school, that's literally their job. At home, it feels to them like it's their job because they want you to become an independent, functional young person. Try and see their feedback as an opportunity to learn more and not as a constant reminder that you are not perfect. You might feel exposed, uncomfortable and like you're not good enough but if you're doing your best, then you are so much more than good enough. Every now and then, you could gently ask your adults to comment on what you do well so that you can do more of that.

BFF rules!
You are going to be around you for your whole life so it would be wise to crack on and learn to love yourself. Whatever your circumstances, you can be the person who treasures you and supports you. Here's how!

What do you do when a friend is feeling sad or worried? I imagine you try to be kind.

Be kind to yourself especially when you're sad, anxious, worried, angry or afraid. Remind yourself of the reasons for these feelings (see Chapter Five) and what you can do about them. Pay yourself compliments when you notice something positive about yourself. It'll give your confidence and self-esteem a boost.

What do you say to a friend when they make a mistake? Maybe something like, 'It's OK to get things wrong, it's what you do afterwards that counts'? From now on, say this to yourself.

You've got the idea – here are the rest of the rules for learning to **LOVE your SELF!**

Respect yourself and know how you expect to be treated by others and by yourself. Don't compromise your values to make someone else feel good at your expense. It's fine to put someone else first occasionally but don't make a habit of it.

Forgive yourself as you would a friend for bad behaviour while being clear about how to avoid it happening in the future.

Encourage yourself every step of the way, every day. Be

your own cheerleader.

Listen to your brain-body and give it what it needs. It will serve you well if you keep it healthy.

Apologise to yourself if you find yourself being unkind to yourself, saying mean things or depriving yourself of the things you need and are entitled to.

Be honest with yourself and don't rely on false certainties or trap yourself into negative beliefs that will limit your happiness and success.

Appreciate yourself for who you are, not what you can do.

Support yourself to achieve your goals by looking after your physical and mental health.

Randomly carry out small acts of self-kindness to yourself – make something lovely, funny, silly or useful and take pleasure in using or looking at it. Go for a walk and listen to the various sounds you hear in the busy or quiet places. Snuggle up and watch a great movie and write a note to yourself to remind you what you like about yourself. Or treat yourself to a long bath and an early night. Or anything that's a treat and you think you'd like.

Spend time on yourself and find time to do good things with good people who you love.

Stand up for yourself and speak out when you need to.

Trust yourself to do your best and be reliable.

These are great tips for helping you to be a great friend to yourself - and to other people.

Stick at it

Which of these BFF rules do you need to get better at when you're dealing with yourself?

Pick one or two and think about or use the sticky notes to write them here. Decide how you are going to introduce them into your life and add anything you need to the notes. Chat it over with a friend or one of your adults.

Healthy relationships

Relationships are important in your life, whether they are with family, friends or people you're romantically attracted to. We are social beings and need our tribe. You have a responsibility to treat others well and you also have a right to be treated well.

Healthy relationships mean we feel safe and trusted and in them we can share affection and physical contact. This creates a hormone called oxytocin which is pumped through your body, making you feel loved and recognised as loveable. This is what makes you feel close to someone and gives you that warm, secure feeling inside.

In any healthy relationship, the connection between you both is based on respect for each other and makes both of you feel good about yourself. That's the same whether your relationship is with your adults and family, a friend or a partner. Respect means that both of you value yourself and each other, you understand the other person's boundaries without putting pressure on them or attempting to control them and you don't tell them what to do. Trust means knowing the other person won't try to hurt, upset or embarrass you on purpose.

Self-control is important even during conflict, which will inevitably arise in most relationships from time to time. Arguments are going to happen because they're a normal, natural part of relationships. However cross or upset you are feeling, it's important to remember to treat the other person as you would want to be treated. Bear in mind that insults and ridiculing are hurtful and unkind behaviours and it can be harder to make up if you've said mean things to each other. Sometimes it's more important to be happy than it is to be right

Even in healthy relationships, you might sometimes feel jealous or envious but if those feelings become so powerful that they make either of you behave unkindly or aggressively, that is a problem that needs to be talked about and resolved calmly. Good communication requires honesty and compromise on both sides and one person should not always have to give in or allow the other their own way all the time. It's perfectly possible to resolve differences in relationships where both of you are prepared and able to discuss, adapt and really listen to the other person.

Unhealthy relationships
The occasional fall-out or cross word doesn't mean a relationship is unhealthy. But if disagreements become a pattern between you both, or anger, controlling behaviour, jealousy, pressure, ridicule, insults or aggression start to surface, you may decide to end the relationship and walk away. Being treated respectfully is what you deserve. Sometimes it's not easy to walk away, depending on who you are falling out with and what their relationship to you is. Talk to a trusted friend or adult and use the websites in the resources section to get help if you are in a difficult relationship and you don't know how to move forward.

However close you may be to a someone, it isn't your job to make them better or happier. You are only responsible for yourself. While it's great to be a good friend, be there for people and let them know about Bob, if they make you feel guilty or start to put pressure on you to fix things for them, you may need to take a break. Chat to someone if you find yourself in this position and remember that your happiness is in your own hands.

Letting go
Sometimes a relationship may end because you or they have decided it no longer suits one of you. Whether it's a family member, a friend or a romantic relationship, this can be painful, confusing and overwhelming. Your adults and friends can comfort you and listen to you, but no one can

go through it for you. Breaking up is hard for you both, but even harder for the person who isn't choosing to end the relationship. Trying to talk about the issues and explaining your feelings is helpful. It might be difficult to imagine your life without that person being close to you and so involved in your day-to-day activities but you will get through it and learn to adapt and adjust, then move forward. Things will change and you will feel stronger. You'll also learn quite a lot about yourself in this situation, too.

"Life is like riding a bicycle. To keep your balance, you must keep moving."

Albert Einstein

To help your brain-body stay as healthy as possible, so you can make the most of every chance to live a life you love, there are things it needs from you every day. It's important to take time to manage your stress and find the time for some self-care. Too much stress can affect your thinking skills and your ability to make good decisions and healthy choices which can make any problems feel and become more difficult to cope with. There are times when stress is unavoidable in the short term or may be out of your control and it's even more important at those points to make an effort to look after yourself as well as you can.

The high five

I've mentioned a few times about taking good care of yourself. Here are five essential things you need to stay healthy and happy, so that you can make the most of your life.

1. **R&R** – Rest and relaxation are essential for your wellbeing and also help you to manage your everyday stress. By taking some time to de-stress and rest, you will increase your ability to cope with things that come. R&R is doing anything you find relaxing, and doing it on purpose for the sake of it, so that you have fun. Pick your favourite calming techniques from Chapter Five and make them a daily habit.

2. **Nutrition** – Viewing food as fuel for your brain-body is a healthy way to keep it energised and strong. This will help you to make good choices most of the time about what you eat without overthinking it.

3. **Hydration** – Water helps keep your brain-body hydrated, and in great shape. A hydrated brain is more efficient at everything it needs to do, including learning, living and loving yourself.

4. **Exercise** – Regular exercise is essential for keeping your brain-body in good working order. It boosts blood circulation and keeps your muscles and organs healthy. You don't have to do a vigorous workout, just walking 20-30 minutes every day is helpful. Exercising in daylight is great as it helps

your brain when it comes to regulating sleep patterns.

5. **Sleep** – You need enough sleep to allow your body to rest and recover from the day, from any injury or illness, and for your brain to clean itself and get rid of waste from the pruned cells, do its filing of everything you've learnt and experienced and manage some dream time (*REM*). As a teenager, you need the most sleep as your brain is working so hard. The ideal amount is about 9-10 hours a night (which is why you love a lie in and struggle to get up for school!).

Sleep sense

Keep a sleep diary for a week. Work out how many hours you get out of the total 63-70 hours you need and see what your shortfall is. Then have a snooze for as long as you choose when you get the opportunity!

An extra note about sleep

Sleep patterns are ruled by a complicated mix of brain signals and hormones. During adolescence, your brain's sense of day and night shifts by a few hours, making it harder to fall asleep until a chemical called melatonin is released. This might be around 11 p.m. or sometimes even later. It can then be hard to wake up and get going in the morning. Some schools start their day later to help out their tired teens.

Not getting enough sleep is called sleep deprivation – something that has been used historically as a form of torture because it's so unpleasant to endure and makes you emotional and irritable, and less able to learn or focus your attention. You could be losing up to three hours of sleep a night which is around 15 hours in the school week. Catch up at the weekends, and tell your adults I said so!

Too little sleep affects your mood and your memory, makes anxiety worse and slows down your brain's development. Studies have shown that it can also make you gain weight.

Did you know?

If you go over something you've learnt in the day just before you fall asleep, it will get wired into your brain more quickly and for longer.

Sleep tips

- Avoid screens in the hour before bed if they are backlit as the light delays the melatonin your brain needs to release so you can fall asleep.

- Spend time in the natural light during the day and in low level light before bed. This helps your brain with its day and night cycles.

- Avoid heavy meals before bed. It can help to have a small snack of carbohydrate and protein – a bowl of oats and milk or vegan milk is ideal.

- Put on some warm socks – if your feet are toasty, it makes you fall asleep more quickly! Try it!

- Develop a routine to wind down – maybe a bath or shower, some relaxing music or read a book in bed.

- Do a relaxation exercise like a safe place meditation, progressive muscle relaxation, body scan or a breathing exercise, such as 3:5 breathing. Keep doing it for 20 minutes or until you're fast asleep.

"Tell me, what is it you plan to do with your one wild and precious life?"

Mary Oliver

Looking after yourself well and showing your brain-body the love it deserves is something you have to regularly remind yourself to do until it becomes a habit. In the Stone Age, they didn't have the luxury of picking and choosing a healthy diet, cutting down on screen time or drinking fewer fizzies. Their lives were simpler and more in tune with nature (but much more dangerous) – sleeping when it was dark, hunting in the daylight, drawing and painting on cave walls with coloured rocks, chalk and charcoal, sitting around fires relaxing, telling stories and singing along together. There were times of high stress and activity when the local lion came looking for a juicy human, and times of calm and rest, with a lot of downtime for the brain to recharge and refresh. Our lives have evolved so much and yet our emotional brain is still back there, sparking fires with a couple of bits of broken flint and a handful of dried out moss. Then, there were few choices about what to do with your life. Now, there's a whole universe of possibilities.

You just have to keep your head (by which I mean thinking brain) while your teen brain is going through its system update.

There are things that young people sometimes find tempting and hard to resist because they feel exciting. You are programmed to be more adventurous in adolescence and to try new things and do new things you wouldn't have done before and which your adults might very much prefer you not to do. In the Stone Age, as you hit your teens you might have chosen to set your sights on bringing down the fiercest lion or the woolliest mammoth to show how strong and capable you were. There would've been quite the thrill in tracking, stalking and hunting your target and then posing for a selfie cave drawing with the new rugs and weekly food haul for your entire family. If you survived it. Nowadays, the thrills are a bit different but can be just as wild – and dangerous for some. When your adults remind you of the dangers, it's because they know that you are looking for things that feel exciting, but they also know, and want you to know, how precious you and your life are. When Bob is in full *hunt or be hunted* mode, you'll act impulsively, taking more risks and sometimes having poor judgment and insight as Bob makes only black and white decisions. They organise the release of the chemicals adrenaline and cortisol which energise you, make you stronger and cause you to feel less pain so you're more likely to act on those impulses.

"*I am my world.*"

Ludwig Wittgenstein

To really **LOVE your SELF!** and make the most of your life, it's important to make sure you get to enjoy a long one by taking care of yourself. Even if you have zero clue right now what to do with your life as an adult, which is fine by the way, knowing that you want to have the best life possible can be a brilliant way of keeping your wilder side under control when the temptations grow too strong. Not everyone feels this pressure but if you do, it's important to know the facts and the risks.

Smoking, vaping, drinking alcohol, taking drugs or hanging out with people who are doing those things can feel exciting. This might be partly because you know your adults wouldn't approve and, depending on your age, you could be breaking the law. Your peers, on the other hand, may be impressed and you may feel more like you fit in because of these choices. Your Bob and their Bob are likely to communicate with one another through your behaviours and may tussle to be top dog, and that can lead to escalating the risk taking to see who can go the furthest – all without the deliberate intention of doing so. It's common to find yourself doing things you wouldn't usually do or that you later regret.

Your adolescent brain is much more receptive than an adult brain to substances like drugs and alcohol, including caffeine and energy drinks, as a result of your dopamine receptors and reward pathway being triggered (see page 95). When you are less in control of your thoughts and behaviour because of substances, you may find yourself in unsafe situations without the awareness to protect yourself.

It's a good idea to work out your own values and boundaries so you don't get pressured into doing anything you don't want to do or find yourself getting caught up in the moment and going total Bob. That's why having a sense of yourself as a future adult can keep you grounded. You're always responsible for your own actions and if something goes wrong, it's you who has to deal with the consequences even if your peers encouraged you into it.

When you're going through tricky times, you may feel you can cover up difficult feelings by using substances but once the effect has worn off, you will feel worse. And repeat. With ever worsening effects. Use this book and the resources in it to find healthy ways to cope with your feelings and you'll stay healthy and feel happier.

Substances could damage your physical health, and mental health conditions like depression or anxiety may get worse or you may be more likely to develop mental illness. The chemicals in substances act like your own dopamine and give you a high for a short time which hijacks your natural feel-good system and distorts it. We know that the illegal drug, cannabis (weed), has a particular effect on the teenage brain that can interfere with its healthy development through the pruning phase in a way it doesn't seem to affect the brains of older people. Paranoia is a common impact of cannabis use in adolescence, perhaps heightening your already over-aware sense of yourself. Other drugs can cause or worsen perception disorders which interfere with how you experience and relate to reality.

If you feel unable to cope without the substance, your life will revolve around getting more of it and you'll start to feel that it is in control of you rather than being something you can choose whether or not to do. This is called addiction. Addiction is hard to break so you'll need to get help if you realise you have developed an addiction.

There are laws to protect you and your health while you're at an age where your brain-body is still growing and developing. These substances have been linked to serious illnesses like cancer and heart disease and you can't buy alcohol or tobacco until you're 18. Buying and selling drugs is illegal. If you're worried about anything, ask for help. Check out the resources section of the book if you need to.

"I am not this hair,
I am not this skin,
I am the soul that lives within."

Rumi

Self-image

Your self-image is how you feel about your appearance, your personal style and your individual attributes such as your hair, your skin, your facial features and other aspects of you that people see when they look at you. It's normal to spend time thinking about and experimenting with 'the look' you want to portray to others and also to yourself. Your self-image may also be part of how you define yourself as an individual or as part of your tribe. It might involve clothing brands or styles, hair colour or styles, make-up, jewellery or other embellishments. Sometimes young people can become fixated on something about their appearance that bothers them which becomes all they can see in the mirror. Your mind can play tricks on you if you decide a particular feature is unattractive or too big, too small, too round, or too... anything. You may struggle with your self-image as you go through changes in your development – there's often a stage where your nose is out of proportion with the rest of your face, for example. It doesn't last long but can be unsettling. Remember what Socrates has taught us? Don't be fooled into believing the first thought you have. Listen to the positive things other people around you are saying to you. The best advice is to find what you like about your appearance and focus on those aspects. As you 'grow into yourself', you get a more balanced sense of your appearance. Above all else, remember that YOU are not your appearance. You are a learning, loving, developing, capable young human with so much more to define you than your appearance. Make sure your self-image takes all those things into account.

Body image

Body image is the term used to explain how we think and feel about ourselves physically, and how we believe others see us. It covers your sense of your body as a whole, including any disabilities or differences in your unique, individual body and how you feel about them. It can take time to come to accept any limitations your body experiences through its unique form, needs, shape or size. Frustration at what your body can and can't do sometimes makes body image a difficult area for young people. Take good care of your body and try to keep it as healthy as you can so that you can explore the possibilities of all the amazing things it can do for you. Wherever possible, focus on how much your body does for you and show it kindness and gratitude.

During the teen years, your body is changing and it can be hard to have a secure sense of it from one day to the next. As I mentioned earlier, you're much more aware of others looking at you, thanks to increased levels of cortisol flooding through you. You've also got new lumps and bumps growing that your brain hasn't yet had time to incorporate into its you-map! As well as affecting your balance and finer movements, this phenomenon can hugely affect your confidence and your ideas about how you look to other people until everything settles down.

In addition, you might be comparing yourself to others around you who are developing in different ways and at different rates and feeling like you're not good enough. Unfortunately, most people, even the ones YOU think look great, are doing this to themselves too. You're also bombarded by photoshopped images of perfect-looking celebrities every time you check out Insta or go on any of your screens. Valuing yourself for all that you are, not what you look like, is the key to good levels of confidence and self-esteem. Using the skills you have learnt to reframe or look at things another way will help you to think about other ways you are valued.

Body positive
Loving yourself requires you to drop the desire for perfection. It's important to care for your body and eat healthily, exercise, drink plenty of water and get enough sleep but different bodies will respond to identical lifestyles differently, according to their genes and environment. You'll have friends who have acne and some who never seem to have any spots, some who are taller than you and some who are shorter than you. You'll know friends who can eat twice what you do and yet stay effortlessly slim, as well has having friends who eat less than you but struggle to manage their weight. Scientists are learning more about these issues all the time and are discovering why there is so much variation in human bodies – one common example of the many we know and are learning about is explained on page 224. What's important is being able to embrace your body, love it, take good care of it and feel confident that it's a good body – it's **YOUR** body and it has just as much right to exist and have fun as anybody else's body.

Your body is a marvel – look at all the things it can do. It heals itself while you sleep. It gets you places. It adapts and grows and bends and makes exciting things possible. How often do you stop and think about how amazing and glorious it is? I'm guessing, like most people, not too often. We take our bodies for granted and tell them constantly what we don't like about them. And yet they carry on carrying us. Showing gratitude and saying kind things to your body should be part of your daily routine. Start today and you'll be glad you did.

Thanking you!

Think of something you love to do, whether it's scoring a goal, finishing a great book, creating the best eyeliner wing or flick, doing an awesome back flip, laying in your cosy bed – or whatever! Decide from now on to always say thank you to yourself every time you do that one thing well. Then add more things to the list.

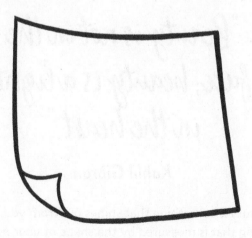

One of the many, relatively recent discoveries about body weight and body fat is a genetic condition called lipoedema. It's thought that 1 in 9 girls (after puberty) and women have it. It rarely affects boys and men but there are other fat disorders that do. However much you exercise, and however healthy your diet is, your body continues to produce a thick layer of fat that covers your legs, hips and sometimes your arms. It can make young women deeply confused because most GPs are not yet trained to recognise it so will assume the fat comes from your lifestyle or that it's because you are developing into a woman. If you notice increased fat on your legs, hips or arms that seems out of proportion to your lifestyle and the rest of your body, search up lipoedema and take the information to your GP. As with any disease, it's important to get on top of it at the early stages as it can become painful and debilitating. You can deal with lipoedema and stop it from progressing and still be body positive!

"Beauty is not in the face; beauty is a light in the heart."

Kahlil Gibran

Your beauty is something that shines out from you, not something that is measured by the shape of your nose, how tall you are, how great you are at things or how popular you are. Everyone has their own opinion on what is appealing. What you find attractive in others will be different from what other people find attractive in you. Often, what attracts you to someone is undefinable – you can't always say what it is about them or why you like them, you just do! Attraction is not always physical – you can be attracted to people for all kinds of reasons.

There are so many forms of beauty and attractiveness, not just the one version that you may have in your mind. YOU are what makes you attractive. If being beautiful were the key to a wonderful life, then every outwardly beautiful person would be blissfully happy every minute of every day and free of any of the stuff you and I worry about. But that's not true, is it? We all have stuff.

If you're unhappy with the way you look, find one or two things about your appearance that you do like and focus on them. Other people will notice them too. Spend as much times as you can around friends and family who make you feel positive about yourself. They value you for many reasons.

Talk to your GP if you are worried about any part of your body or if you're feeling overwhelmed about your body image.

Body Dysmorphia
You know how Bob can make you believe things that aren't true? Like, in my case, that an electric toothbrush buzzing was

a threat to life? I know it was daft but it felt very real to me and as though my life depended on keeping well away from the buzzing. Sometimes your pruning brain gets things very wrong and distorts what you see, the way my ears distorted what I heard.

Body dysmorphia is a perception disorder that can make you very unhappy. It means you don't see your real reflection in the mirror or the real shape or size of parts of your body, or your body as a whole and it can happen to anyone. Other people will not see what you see and won't be able to understand what you're experiencing, because you look completely fine. It's like an optical illusion where your eyes play a cruel trick on you to see the things you're most worried about seeing. You will see yourself as ugly or fat and might not believe people when they say nice things about you. If you experience body dysmorphia, talk to your adults and get support.

The eyes have it
Look at these optical illusions – are the lines the same length or are they different? When you've decided, measure them to find out for sure.

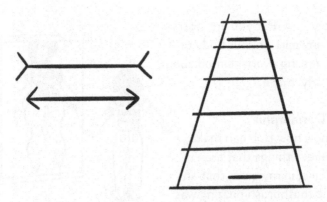

There are so many things to love about you. Fill this heart with ways you can learn to **LOVE your SELF!** AND things you DO love about yourself. Ask other people for ideas and their reasons for loving you, and add those as well.

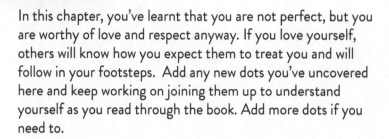

Go dotty!

In this chapter, you've learnt that you are not perfect, but you are worthy of love and respect anyway. If you love yourself, others will know how you expect them to treat you and will follow in your footsteps. Add any new dots you've uncovered here and keep working on joining them up to understand yourself as you read through the book. Add more dots if you need to.

- E.g. I need to remember that I deserve respect and I should not always put others first.

- _____

- _____

- _____

Get connected!

Connect these dots – are you loving how precious this part of the picture is, yet? It's something that is being reclaimed and will be staying where it belongs...

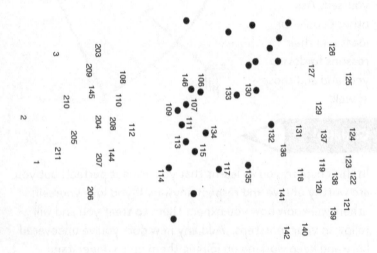

The CHOOSE YOU! Process

RECLAIM IT!

It's time to **RECLAIM IT!** Write down the ways you can **LOVE your SELF!** with the things you named, claimed, reframed and tamed in the process boxes.

If this chapter has given you something else to work on that didn't surface in the previous section, then plan to **RECLAIM IT!** now by adding it to the box so you can come back to the process in the future and work on it.

Remember – always keep to the same box number for each choice so you can track its progress as you use **The CHOOSE YOU! Process.**

I RECLAIM IT!
E.g. I can choose to try to understand what others mean instead of assuming they're criticising me.
1
2
3
4
5

Keep reading and find out in Chapter Seven how to **BE your SELF!** and start living with **NO SHAME!**

CHAPTER SEVEN

NO SHAME!

BE YOUR SELF!

This chapter will:

1. Focus on the final **NO SHAME!** section of **The CHOOSE YOU! Process**

2. Help you be proud to be **YOU!**

3. Understand aspects of yourself that feel key to your own identity

4. Remind you that your body belongs to you and you say what happens to it

5. Explain how individual differences are what make you unique and glorious

6. Show you how you can be your own **HERO** thanks to your attitude, gratitude and latitude

7. Complete **The CHOOSE YOU! Process** and finally reveal the enigmatic dot-to-dot puzzle

8. Lead on to the resources section, full of useful websites and helplines

> *"To be yourself in a world that is constantly trying to make you something else is the greatest accomplishment."*
>
> **Ralph Waldo Emerson**

In this final chapter, we'll look at how to own your identity and feel proud of who you are. You don't need to feel pressure to hurry to 'become' you or make huge decisions – you've been you from the day you were conceived. Like everyone else, you are not a finished product and you'll be changing all the time throughout this busy period of your life. When you are 104 years old, you'll still be changing. Developing an honest sense of yourself is a good indicator that you're moving in the right direction. That's what you've been doing the whole time you've been reading this book.

 I am the one and only

You are an individual and you have the right to define yourself, or not define yourself, however you wish. **BE your SELF!** and know there is **NO SHAME!** in that. You get to decide who you are and what matters to you. You are worthy of love, friendship, respect and happiness. No one has the right to make you feel less than them, or than anyone else.

At the same time, you have a responsibility to behave in ways that ensure you treat others well and are considerate and respectful, regardless of your differences. People have equal value, however they do or don't identify themselves. What people choose to do and how they behave, on the other hand, is an important factor in whether you feel comfortable around them.

Some emotions can get in the way of your confidence to **BE your SELF!** Shame and guilt are particularly unpleasant feelings which can creep up on anyone and make you feel you don't deserve to enjoy yourself. Read about them here so you can conquer them when they pop up.

Shame and guilt
Guilt is the feeling you get when you think you've done something wrong. Everyone makes mistakes, gets things wrong or upsets other people from time to time and it's normal to feel guilty when that happens. Forgiving yourself and asking for forgiveness from anyone who was affected by your actions helps you to learn from what happened. It can take other people a bit of time to accept your apology but you can make amends for what you did and move on from the guilty feelings. If those guilty feelings stick around, they can get in the way of your happiness and stop you from being yourself. Talk to someone you trust if this happens. There are lots of resources at the back of the book to support you in finding someone to talk to.

Shame is the feeling you get when you think there's something about YOU that isn't good enough or as it should be. You might feel you're different or want to be different from what others expect of you. Shame eats away at your sense of self and steals your confidence, individuality and self-esteem. It can be very difficult to cope with and might dominate your thinking on an everyday basis. With your invisible audience hanging around you, you can feel exposed and as though everyone can see all the things you don't like about yourself or that you believe make you a bad person. They can't. It's not true. Use **The CHOOSE YOU! Process** on anything that makes you feel negatively about yourself. There are spare process grids at the back of this book to use if this chapter throws up some beliefs you hadn't identified or didn't want to think about until now. When you avoid thinking about difficult things, you're feeding the negative neural networks and that keeps you trapped. Set yourself free and move forward. You deserve happiness.

You are good enough. You are unique. You can learn to be proud to **BE your SELF!** and live with **NO SHAME!** – that's what this chapter is all about. If any feelings of shame stick around, talk to someone you trust or use the resources in this book. They're included precisely because most people find this stuff hard and I want you to be free of whatever is keeping you prisoner in your own mind.

"Why do you stay
in prison, when the door
is so wide open?"

Rumi

Proud to be YOU!

Fill these sticky notes with things you are proud of in yourself. These might be personality traits, achievements, physical attributes or anything at all that makes you proud to be you.

Identify any of your choices that you know make other people proud of you as well. Maybe highlight, underline or tick them.

Recall a really proud moment in your life from as far back as you can remember. Visualise it happening like watching a movie in your mind. Then rewind it and watch it again, looking for subtle clues on your face in the movie that show how happy you felt.

Read these statements and tick what applies to you	Never true	Sometimes true	Always true
1 I believe in myself			
2 I can say what I'm good at			
3 I'm proud of who I am			
4 I deserve to be happy			
5 I'm important to my friends and family			
6 People listen to my ideas			

If you have ticked mostly **never true**, talk to someone or work out how to improve your self-pride. Maybe the websites at the back of the book will help you identify ways to feel more proud of yourself.

"Be yourself; everyone else is already taken."

Oscar Wilde

You're allowed to be proud of who you are, of the ways in which you are different and the ways you are similar to others. You're a one-off mix of cells, DNA and experiences so you'll never be exactly the same as another person. Even twins have differences, and so do triplets, quadruplets and all the other -lets!

As you've gone through life until now, you've gathered your own collection of likes, dislikes, preferences and tastes. You'll have tribe loyalties based on the things that interest you, like music, sport, films and all the other things you're into. These things can feel really important and you may want to define yourself by the groups you are part of. These groups, or tribes, may change frequently as you mature and learn more about yourself and the world.

Some other ways you might identify with, or feel different from, peers and friends are to do with your mind, body, gender and sexuality but these aspects may feel more fixed to you. Gender and sexuality are often talked about as the same thing but they are different.

Some young people are very clear from an early age how they feel about their gender and who they are attracted to, some aren't sure, some don't have particularly strong feelings about it and some don't want to think about it. However you feel about these things, it can be confusing and scary, messy and complicated and these feelings can make you believe you're not 'normal'. There is no normal. Even if you're surrounded by people who look like they've got it all sorted out, that's not true. Socrates has taught us about this stuff, right? What looks like fact, very often isn't. All dogs are NOT amphibians.

I'll be using a lot of terms in this section of **CHOOSE YOU!** so to make it easier, you'll find the relevant definitions here instead of in the glossary at the back of the book. I've put the terms in **bold** letters to help you if you want to search up more about them.

Gender

At the time of your birth, medical staff will record your gender as female or male based on your reproductive organs. People who feel comfortable with their assigned gender are referred to as **cisgender** or **cis**. A baby born with physical attributes that don't conform to society's assumptions of what constitutes male or female is recorded as **intersex**. Parents may raise the baby according to the gender they decide on for their child and medical staff may have an influence on the parents' choice. This may be different from how the child identifies later in life and they may choose a different gender identity. It is important that the young person is supported to do this at a time and pace that suits them. It's important not to feel rushed into decisions and to have access to all the information you need.

If you are cisgender, you may find you feel frustrated by others' ideas of what each gender can, can't, should or shouldn't do. Plenty of role models have broken down these barriers – maybe there's someone you admire for doing exactly this? Look for others around you who inspire you to achieve your dreams and goals and follow in their footsteps. Or create your own footsteps for others to follow in and be a trailblazer!

You might feel **non-binary**, which means you don't identify as either male or female, or feel you're both, or neither. Some people feel **gender fluid** and do not want to be confined to any single definition of their gender. It's always up to you to decide and there are no time limits around your decisions. You can also change your mind as and when you like, too.

You might be sure your assigned gender is wrong for you, or prefer the company of another gender and identify more with them than with your assigned gender but feel unsure what that means. If those feelings don't change as you get older and start causing you distress and discomfort, you may be experiencing **gender dysphoria**. If you feel you have the wrong reproductive organs for who you really are, you might identify as **transgender** or **trans**. Sometimes trans people want to change their body to match their gender identity and sometimes they don't want to. The choice is very much an individual one. Whether or not you feel transgender, you may want to dress in clothes you feel match your identity.

You might worry how others in your family or community will react if you choose not to express yourself as cis, and you may not know how to start the conversation with them. You'll need support from a trusted adult to help you with this, not just for coming to terms with your feelings which may be very strong and perhaps bewildering, but also to get advice and guidance from professionals who can help you explore any next steps you wish to take.

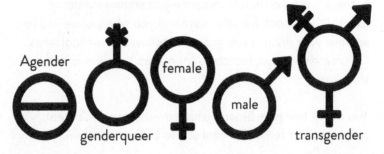

Sexuality

Sexuality is who you are physically and/or romantically attracted to. Sexual attraction happens when you find someone physically attractive and may include feeling you want to have sex or sexual contact with them. Sexuality is as diverse as all other human identities. Women who are attracted to men, and men who are attracted to women identify as **heterosexual** or **straight**. Men who are attracted to other men identify as **homosexual** or **gay**. Women who are attracted to other women sometimes choose these terms, too.

Sexualities other than heterosexual, and gender identities other than cisgender are covered by the acronym **LGBTQIA+**. This acronym stands for **lesbian**, **gay**, **bisexual**, **transgender**, **questioning** (or **queer**), **intersex**, **Asexual**, **Aromantic** and more.

Many of these definitions are used as umbrella terms by some. Individuals may find they identify with none, one or more of these definitions. If you want to explore these or other terms, see the listing for Stonewall in the resources section.

Lesbian – a woman who is attracted to romantic and/or sexual relationships with other women.

Gay – a man who is attracted to romantic and/or sexual relationships with other men; some women define themselves as gay rather than lesbian. Some non-binary people may also identify with this term.

Bisexual – someone who is attracted to romantic and/or sexual relationships with more than one gender. This umbrella can also include other identities such as pansexual/omnisexual, which refer to someone whose romantic and/or sexual attraction towards others is not limited by sex or gender.

Transgender – someone who identifies as a gender other than the gender assigned at birth.

Questioning – someone in the process of working out their identity.

Queer – someone who finds other labels too restrictive may choose to identify as queer. It was once considered a demeaning slur but has been reclaimed by some as an umbrella term for their identity.

Intersex – someone born with male and female reproductive organs or with biological attributes that don't fit the typical definitions of male or female bodies.

Asexual – someone who isn't sexually attracted to anyone, but may have romantic attractions.

Aromantic – someone who isn't romantically attracted to anyone, but may have sexual attractions.

+ Plus – + is a way to ensure all identities are recognised because there are as many identities as there are people, and not everyone will feel that they fit within one or any of these prescribed definitions.

Your body, your rules

To **BE your SELF!** is to feel you have the **right** to be the person you want to be. That includes being in charge of your own body and only using it the way you want to. No one else has the right to say what happens to your body or to use your body for their own needs.

If you are unwell, medical staff will take care of you and do what's necessary in an emergency. In a non-emergency situation, you should be asked for your permission and have everything explained so you can make decisions about your treatment.

Sexual attraction may well be becoming more important for you at this stage of your development. You'll probably start to think about sex, relationships and your sexuality more often or in more depth. Not everyone is interested in sex, romance and attraction. You can be romantically attracted to someone without wanting to have sex with them, or you may feel sexually attracted to someone you can't or don't want to have a relationship with.

Sometimes your sexual feelings may be quite strong which can be exciting and confusing at the same time. When you're ready to have sex, you should expect it to be respectful, enjoyable and pleasurable. You have the right to be able to say no and to stop at any time. You can't legally agree to have sex under the age of 16, whatever your sexuality or gender. Make sure you talk to a trusted adult or check out the resources if anything to do with your body or sex worries you.

Sexting
Think, think and think again!

Sexting is difficult territory. In the heat of the moment, it might seem exciting and fun to send sexual images but remember that when you're feeling like this, you may not always be able to make good decisions. Don't send anything you wouldn't want your adults to see because if things go wrong, that's something that is very likely to happen. Once you've sent a picture or video, it can go anywhere and resurface later in your life.

If someone is pressuring you to send something you don't want to send, seek help from someone you trust.

To have or send sexual pictures or videos, including selfies, you must legally be over the age of 18 and the people in them must be over 18 as well.

If something goes wrong, talk to an adult who you trust. It'll feel difficult and you may feel guilty, ashamed, embarrassed or frightened but it's a mistake you will learn from. Forgive yourself – it's happened before and it will happen again. If a naked picture of you ends up on a website and you're under 18, you can report it to the website to have it removed or you can contact the Internet Watch Foundation anonymously (see the resources section in this book).

Porn

There's a very good chance you will encounter porn online. If you see anything that upsets you, you can move on. If you want to report it, you can. Porn is not designed to represent real-life sex. It's idealised and isn't concerned with the enjoyment of the people involved. Real sex will look and feel quite different from what you see online. You should not be expected to behave like the actors. Only do what you want to do. You must legally be 18 to access porn in any format.

Be safe online

- You have the right to feel safe online and you have a responsibility to treat others well. You are responsible for what you post, say and do online.

- You won't always know who you're really talking to so be as careful as you would be in real life.

- Someone who cares about you would never ask you to do anything harmful or dangerous, including online or via technology.

- Never share your personal information with someone you don't know in person, like your full name, address or phone number.

- Use privacy settings to protect your information.

- If you get unpleasant messages or you're being bullied, get help. Don't believe their threats.

- Delete, block and report anything that makes you uncomfortable. You can easily report posts or pictures on social media sites.

"I believe in standardising automobiles. I do not believe in standardising human beings."

Albert Einstein

This is ME!

You'll have plenty in common with your friends, family and peers, but you will also have individual differences. These are things about you such as your traits, your values, your personality, your brain-body and all its quirks, wirings and functions. From your hair to your shoe size, your kindness to your learning skills, and your thinking brain to your Bob, these individual differences are specific to your sense of self and will affect how you see yourself and the world around you. They'll affect how positive you feel and how you react to adversity but I hope I've been able to show you that these things are not stuck, there is not one truth and you can **CHOOSE** how you'd like to feel, adapt, react and grow.

There are many ways we show our individual differences. Reading this book and doing some of the activities will have helped you to identify some of the quirks of your individual brain-body. You may have known and understood some of them already. It's important to embrace your individual differences and be proud of what makes you unique. That's not always easy when you are very aware of yourself and how you fit in with the rest of the world. You might prefer to be the same as everyone else and not stand out. That's OK too, as long as you remember these three things: that you're not the same as everyone else, everyone else isn't the same as everyone else and everyone else isn't the same as you!

List some random facts about anything at all to do with yourself on this checklist.

FACT	FACT

Tick off any facts you know also apply to someone else. Leave unticked the facts that only apply to you.

Maybe you could repeat this task with someone else in mind and write random facts about them too, ticking off any that are shared.

Not all brain types think the same way. In Chapter Two, I described brains as being either neurotypical or neurodiverse. This description recognises that all brains are great, just as they are, and are of equal value. Because neurotypical brains are in the majority, it can make life harder to have a neurodiverse brain as the majority tend to set the way things are organised in the world. That's the same for any differences between humans in the remarkable human race such as being left-handed or shorter than average. It's important, whatever your brain type, that you are aware of its advantages as well as any disadvantages or differences you feel exist. There are key thinking differences and neurodiverse brains can sometimes make their owners find some aspects of learning more challenging, while finding they have unusual abilities or clarity in other areas of learning. Without diverse brains, the whole circle of human existence would be incomplete and some inventions, systems, machines, medicines or works of art would never have been created because neurotypical brains do not always think in ways that would have led to these innovations.

Knowing how your own brain thinks helps you to understand yourself and to celebrate its uniqueness and special abilities, building on these to do well in ways that matter to you. Sometimes people go through their lives experiencing the challenges of neurodiversity without realising why they find things so difficult, and without having discovered or being shown the positive aspects of their differences. If neurodiversity is not picked up in childhood, it can sometimes lead to years of confusion. That's a situation that can damage self-esteem and can make you believe there is something 'wrong' with you because you don't know why your thoughts work a particular way that appears to be different to other people you know. If neurodiversity is not picked up in childhood, it can lead to a lifetime of confusion and damage to self-esteem.

If any of this sounds like you, read the descriptions in the grid below. Talk to your adults if anything seems like it could apply to you and you want to explore it further. Without a diagnosis, neurodiverse people can often believe they don't fit in, just because they don't seem to think like everyone else around them. If you feel you might be neurodiverse, you don't have to get a diagnosis – that is a purely personal preference to be decided between you and your adults. What matters is understanding yourself and choosing how you want to respond to your own individual challenges. The details in this grid are quite simplistic but should give you a starting point to think it over and do your own research. Some of the websites in the resources section are useful for this, too.

	Benefits	Difficulties
ADHD	creativity, focus, energy and passion	sustaining concentration
ASD (Autism/Asperger's)	fine detail processing and memory	problems with social and emotional communication
Dyslexia/Dysgraphia	visual thinking, creativity, 3D mechanical skills	spelling, reading, putting thoughts into writing
Dyscalculia	verbal skills, innovative creativity and thinking	understanding number representations, maths
Dyspraxia	verbal skills, empathy and intuition	physical co-ordination and organisation
Tourette's Syndrome	observational skills, cognitive control, creativity	involuntary face and/or movements and sounds

Sensory processing

How your brain-body handles the information that comes from the outside through your senses, along with all the information from the inside of you such as emotions and bodily sensations, is known as sensory processing. All brains have to process, or turn what they see, smell, touch, hear, taste and feel into information that can be used to form an appropriate response in any given situation. For example, in a fire drill, the bells will ring loudly and you'll be expected to calmly go outside to a meeting point. Your brain-body needs to take in the information from the bells, understand what it means and form an appropriate response to keep you safe and fit in with others' expectations. For some people, with or without a neurodiverse brain (although it's more common with a neurodiverse brain), this can be especially hard and they can feel hugely overwhelmed as though they are having a meltdown, where things stop making sense temporarily and they have no idea how to respond. This can happen occasionally to anyone but if it becomes a common event, you may be experiencing a sensory processing disorder. This means it's tricky to stay level-headed, calm and rational when your brain-body perceives the information as a threat. So, some people feel lights are too bright, places are too crowded, sounds are too loud and all sorts of other 'too much' feelings which leaves them feeling unable to cope. The brain-body isn't able to organise the information that's bombarding it into a helpful response so the only thing you can do then is run away, hide, explode or sit it out until something changes.

There are effective treatments for sensory processing problems and, neurodiverse or neurotypical, you can learn to manage the information better most of the time.

Bullying

History is full of people using their power to feel better about themselves by making others feel bad. Bullying often focuses on things that are different between the bully and the victim. Animals also use this dominance behaviour and fight to be leader of the pack or in the top dog's group. Bullying is the deliberate and repeated use of power by a person or group to hurt or upset others and usually fits into these four forms:

Verbal: name-calling, repeated teasing, mocking, insults or threats.

Physical: pushing or hurting, damaging, hiding or stealing belongings, using their body to intimidate, making a person do things with their body that makes them feel uncomfortable.

Emotional: exclusion, control, mocking or belittling a person or placing undeserved blame and spreading rumours.

Cyber: using technology to bully, sending unwanted, embarrassing or upsetting messages, spreading private chats or photos, making threats, being offensive about an individual or their family via technology.

Bullying is never acceptable. If you experience bullying, whether it's to do with your identity, appearance, individual differences or anything else, speak to a trusted adult and get help from the many organisations listed in this book. If you realise that you are bullying others because of how you view them, remember how much harm you might do them and STOP – think about what is behind your behaviour and get help to stop if you need it. You may find other people experience your actions as bullying when you haven't intended them to be – be prepared to listen to their view and make sure you are treating them as you would like to be treated. That is often a great way to assess the impact of your actions on other people. And don't forget about TRUCE. Flip back to page 99 if you need a reminder about this!

> *"Beauty begins the moment you decide to be yourself."*
>
> **Coco Chanel**

Well done on getting this far, unless you're like me and you started at the back to see what happens before you read the rest. In which case you're in for a treat as you've got the whole book to go yet! (P.S. – the frog did it!)

Everything I've said up until now can be summed up in three words. Attitude, gratitude and latitude. Hang on! You mean I've written over 50,000 words and I only needed to write three? Well, no. (Phew!) It's a summing up, a way of remembering all the valuable lessons of challenging your negative thoughts and beliefs, Bob, relaxation, being kind to yourself. And amphibians.

Let me break it down for you.

Attitude

A positive attitude is a way of looking at things that grows helpful neural networks, as you know only too well by now. It's all about how you **CHOOSE** to look at things. When you can **BE your SELF!**, your positive attitude to life will be hugely helpful to you. People are often very attracted to friendships with someone who has a positive attitude because it feels good to be thought well of and in the company of someone who views the world as an exciting and enjoyable place.

Your positive attitude makes others feel good about themselves when they are with you because they see your positivity reflected back at them and their Bob feels fabulous basking in your sunshine. And your Bob feels great spending time with them, too. If you expect the best outcomes **and** put in the effort to achieve this, your attitude and relationships will keep gaining in positivity. The best advice for improving your attitude is to focus on **being curious**. It helps you to be more creative, confident and resilient. If you approach life as a series of opportunities to discover the how and why of everything rather than just the what, you'll open up your thinking and with it your possibilities.

Gratitude

Being thankful allows you to focus on the things that are helping you, encouraging you or teaching you things. Gratitude to yourself and to others makes you stop and realise just how much good stuff is going on around you, for you, by you and within you. Be grateful for the tough moments. Some of your best learning comes from the hardest lessons, in life and in school, and it might sound crazy to be grateful for those things, but try it! It boosts your world view and your confidence. Mistakes will feel more like the experiments they really are. Be grateful to your mistakes – they are the evidence that you are one of a kind and you are making progress.

Enjoying the process of progress is something we don't always take the time to do, as we can be so fixed on the outcome. When the latest cars, trainers or technological devices are designed, the creators don't sit down with one idea and get on with it, stop for lunch, carry on a bit and then at the end of the day have the thing ready and working faultlessly. When I sat down to write this book, I didn't start at page one and keep writing until the last page and then hit print. Movies aren't filmed in the right order with each scene running smoothly one after the other and then shown to the actors before they go home that night. All these things are edited, tested, cut out, scrapped, added back in, changed and are redone over and over and over again. And then spell-checked! They are all part of a **process** of refining, retrying and re-doing. I made loads of mistakes writing this book and that's OK because – trust me, I'm a doctor! – mistakes are the best opportunities. They make it clear what needs to be changed, improved or thought about differently. And I wasn't on my own – I had my editor, designer and illustrator to help me when organising the words in my head felt like herding cats. Be grateful for the successful and the unsuccessful, for the people who help you along and show you other ways of thinking, being and doing. Completing **The CHOOSE YOU! Process** could help you develop your gratitude towards yourself as you uncover those dots and pick out how they all connect to the bigger picture of you.

Latitude

Latitude is the freedom you give yourself to think or act beyond what is easy, predictable, effortless or limiting. It's about choosing to run with the pack or start your own pack, to blend in or stand out. All options are valid. Decide to free yourself up, to retrain and upgrade Bob and get back in control even during your own system update. Give yourself permission to **CHOOSE your SELF!**, **KNOW your SELF!**, **SHOW your SELF!**, **GROW your SELF!**, **HELP your SELF!**, **LOVE your SELF!** and **BE your SELF!**

You are ready.

Now you have the attitude, gratitude and latitude, you can be your own HERO and push yourself on to accomplish your own goals, however you define them. Decide what YOU want to do to help you **BE your SELF!**

A **HERO** has four main qualities – do what you can to grow these qualities and use them every day.

Hope – you believe that good things are possible, and they can and do happen ☐

Energy – you put effort into making good things happen ☐

Resilience – you believe you can overcome obstacles and keep trying ☐

Optimism – you believe in your own power to succeed ☐

You can **CHOOSE** to be your own **HERO** and put a great big tick next to all of these. What are waiting for? You've just read a whole book about how to **CHOOSE your SELF!**

YOU'RE ALREADY MY HERO. NOW GO AND BE YOURS.

It's time for you to step into your own shoes and **BE your SELF!**

Go dotty!

In this chapter, you've learnt to be proud of who you are and why it matters that you feel unique. Add any new dots you've uncovered here and use the blank process boxes at the back of the book to work on them if you want to. Add more dots if you need to.

> ● E.g. I don't always feel sure about myself and what I want.
>
> ● _____
>
> ● _____
>
> ● _____

Connect all these dots and you'll finally be able to make sense
of the bigger picture. You've been grappling in the dark on
these puzzles until now but you've achieved something massive
reaching this point.

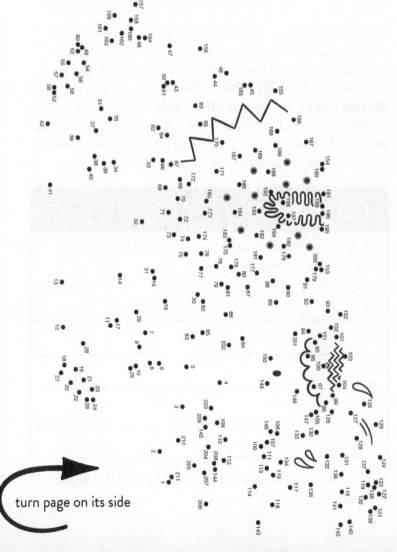

turn page on its side

255

The CHOOSE YOU! Process

NO SHAME!

It's time to live with **NO SHAME!** Write some encouraging words for yourself in the last boxes of the things you've named, claimed, reframed, tamed and reclaimed. And then live it. You are truly glorious, just as you **CHOOSE** to be.

If this chapter has given you something else to work on that didn't surface in the previous section, then why not use the spare blank grids and boxes at the back of this book and go through the whole **CHOOSE YOU! Process** on it so you can **BE your SELF!** and live with **NO SHAME!** You can revisit this anytime you need to and you know you can always **CHOOSE your SELF!** There's no need to re-read the whole book each time, just recap any sections as required.

NO SHAME!
E.g. I'm sensitive, unique and caring and I'm learning to understand myself
1
2
3
4
5

That's it! You've completed **The CHOOSE YOU! Process.**
Well done!

"As you start to walk on the way, the way appears."

Rumi

Making your way through life being yourself and feeling proud of who you are isn't always easy. I'm not sure it's even often easy. Your life as a teen is full of challenges, from your inner world and from the outside world. This book has highlighted a lot of the reasons for those challenges and, hopefully, provided some relief, solutions, connections, questions and ways forward. You've seen how to understand the way your brain works and sometimes reverts to the way things were in the Stone Age.

It's important to say, at this point, that you won't always feel happy. Don't despair when those times come and don't feel you've got to be on top of the world all the time. The view from up there is astonishing and incomparable, and it's a wonderful place to be because you can see far and wide and notice things you'd never spot from anywhere else – as a pilot, I know this to be completely true (sshhh, Socrates – I KNOW that I know nothing!).

But the air's thin up there so it wouldn't do to stay there all the time. Other views of the world are just as valid. Have you ever stood at the edge of the ocean, looked out at the vast blue waters and been curious about what lies beneath? Or sat at the bottom of a tree and looked up into the sky through the branches and leaves and considered how the tiniest of insects can reach the uppermost branches, or how many stars are up there in the universe even when they can't be seen? Or opened a book and found yourself proving that all dogs are amphibians? There's a phenomenal wonder in those things too that will help you learn other dimensions and show you depths, heights and widths full of possibility. And life. And a little bit of philosophy.

Without the odd drop of sadness, or any other painful emotion, the marvellous would become mundane and you'd stop being amazed by the diversity of your own experience. And your own SELF! It will rain on you sometimes. In the words of the great American country singer-songwriter philosopher, Dolly Parton:

"The way I see it, if you want the rainbow, you gotta put up with the rain."

If the odd drop becomes a puddle, you need to ask for help.

So, there'll be times when you don't feel like you know yourself or want to show or grow yourself. It may feel hard to help yourself, love yourself or be proud to be you. You are programmed above all else to adapt and survive. Bob's job is serious stuff. Guiding Bob with your thinking brain and your attitude, gratitude and latitude will reveal your true inner **HERO**.

By completing **The CHOOSE YOU! Process** on anything you feel needs attention, you'll see what and where your dots are. You'll learn how to connect them and how to keep building and discovering yourself, so you can thrive with your tribe and with your **SELF!**

If you can keep growing those positive neural networks, you'll have a skill that will last a lifetime. And you'll have a real advantage in moving forward to become the unique, incredible and happy teenager **YOU CHOOSE** to be!

GO FOR IT.
BE YOU.
I BELIEVE IN
YOU!

"The privilege
of a lifetime
is to become
who you truly are."

Carl Gustav Jung

It's always a good idea to talk to one of your adults about anything that is bothering you if you can. If for any reason that feels too difficult, these organisations are there for you. Sometimes a situation can feel massive and because of all the brain tricks you've read about in this book, you can be convinced you're the exception and even these organisations won't be able to help. Or you might worry they'll be shocked by what you have to say – they won't. They've heard every imaginable problem, will not judge you and they all offer a confidential service. Don't struggle on by yourself. Get help. You deserve to be happy.

Childline

0800 1111

www.childline.org.uk

Information online for loads of issues. Free, confidential help and advice about any worry you have whenever you need it, 24/7. For all young people up to age 19. Phone or online chat, whatever you prefer.

Young Minds

www.youngminds.org.uk

Text YM to 85258

Mental health and wellbeing information, advice and help for young people. Loads of information on the website and a crisis text-line available 24/7 across the UK if you are experiencing a mental health crisis. If you've involved one of your adults, there's a helpline for them if they need help or advice to know how to support you.

Young Minds Parent Helpline
www.youngminds.org.uk
0808 802 5544
Mon-Fri 9:30 a.m. to 4 p.m. – free in the UK
Advisers will listen to your concerns and questions to help you to understand your child's behaviour and give you practical advice on where to go next. If you need further help, they'll refer you to a specialist e.g. psychotherapist, psychiatrist, psychologist or mental health nurse within seven days.

Mind
www.mind.org.uk
0300 123 3393
Text: 86463
For better mental health. Information on a range of topics and they'll look for details of help and support in your own area.
Call weekdays 9 a.m. to 6 p.m.

The Samaritans
www.samaritans.org
116 123
Email: jo@samaritans.org
Listening and support for anyone who needs it.
Contact 24 hours a day, 365 days a year – calls and emails are free and confidential. If you need a response immediately, it's best to call on the phone.

SANE Helpline

www.sane.org.uk

0300 304 7000

SANE's helpline is a national telephone helpline seven days a week for anyone coping with mental illness, including concerned relatives or friends.

Stonewall

www.youngstonewall.org.uk

0800 0502020

For all young lesbian, gay, bi and trans people – as well as those who are questioning – UK and abroad. Helping you know you're not alone. Empowering all young people, regardless of their sexual orientation or gender identity, to campaign for equality and fair treatment for LGBTQ+ people, and act against discrimination.

For information on terms and definitions, see www.stonewall.org.uk/help-advice/glossary-terms

National Autistic society

www.autism.org.uk

UK charity for autistic people and their families. Helping transform lives, change attitudes and create a society that works for autistic people.

Tourette's Action

www.tourettes-action.org.uk

0300 777 8427

Online support for anyone affected by Tourette's and an advice section specifically for young people.

BEAT Eating Disorders

www.beateatingdisorders.org.uk

Youthline 0808 801 0711

Seeking to end the pain and suffering caused by eating disorders. BEAT are a champion, guide and friend to anyone affected, giving individuals experiencing an eating disorder and their loved ones a place where they feel listened to, supported and empowered.

Ditch the Label

www.ditchthelabel.org

An international anti-bullying charity with lots of free online articles and advice.

The Mix

www.themix.org.uk

0808 808 4994

Online support service for under 25s. Free helpline, 24/7 crisis text messaging service, 1-2-1 telephone counselling and a database of services to help you with your worries or issues.

National Bullying Helpline UK

www.nationalbullyinghelpline.co.uk

0845 22 55 787

Anti-bullying organisation that helps adults and children and provides support with bullying in the home, community, playground or workplace.

FRANK

www.talktofrank.com
0300 1236600
Text 82111
FRANK gives honest information about drugs on their website. Offers advice through the phone line, text or email.

Internet Watch Foundation

https://report.iwf.org.uk
If there are sexual images online of you or anyone else under 18, you can anonymously report them here to have them taken down.

Law Stuff

https://lawstuff.org.uk
The Law Stuff website provides free, reliable legal information to children and young people on a range of topics such as education, family, sex, online safety, drugs, your rights and loads of other important subjects. LawStuff is run by Coram Children's Legal Centre, which provides detailed information both over the phone and online.

Youth Access

www.youthaccess.org.uk
020 8772 9900
Young people's information, advice and counselling services. Information about services you can access, up-to-date links and contact information for national helplines for all sorts of youth issues.

Health for teens

www.healthforteens.co.uk

Wide range of information and support for teen issues. Love your body, love yourself, #lovehealth.

Self Harm UK

www.selfharm.co.uk

Dedicated to self-harm recovery, insight and support. Online support for mental health and wellbeing.

Papyrus UK

papyrus-uk.org

0800 068 4141

pat@papyrus-uk.org

Confidential suicide prevention advice and support for any young person feeling they are not coping with life or who are worried about someone else.

Winston's wish

https://help2makesense.org

08088 020 021

An organisation that helps young people and families after the death of someone important to you. Bereavement and grief support. Online resources and information plus a helpline and messaging service.

NSPCC

www.nspcc.org.uk
Advice and support from NSPCC who fight to keep
children and young people safe from abuse.

We Are With You (formerly Addaction)

www.wearewithyou.org.uk
National health charity helping people and families to
overcome problems with addiction, alcohol, drugs, poor
mental health and self-harm. Free confidential webchat
online.

CALM

www.thecalmzone.net
0800 58 58 58
The Campaign Against Living Miserably (CALM) is leading
a movement against suicide and is for anyone at crisis point.
Free and confidential helpline and webchat. Support if
you're feeling suicidal or if you've been bereaved by suicide.

You can get in touch with me via my website
www.drsharie.com or by emailing
askdrsharie@drsharie.com.

Quotes

In order of appearance:

Jobs, Steve 2005, 'Steve Jobs' 2005 Stanford Commencement Address', Stanford, 12 June. Available at: https://www.youtube.com/watch?v=UF8uR6Z6KLc (Accessed 18 February 2020)

Hebb, Donald 1949, The Organization of Behavior, Oxford, UK: Taylor & Francis, Psychology Press.

Vonnegut, Kurt 1992, Mother Night, London, UK: Penguin, Vintage Classics. (Original work published 1962).

Frank, Anne 2007, The Diary of a Young Girl, 2007, London, UK: Penguin. (Original work published 1952).

Angelou, Maya 2020, 'I've learned that people will forget what you said...' posted on Twitter, 26 April. Available at https://twitter.com/DrMayaAngelou/status/1254479066759118856 (Accessed: 8 June 2020)

Thunberg, Greta 2019, No One Is Too Small to Make a Difference, London, UK: Penguin.

Dweck, Carol 2013, Mindset: The New Psychology of Success, New York, US: Ballantine Books.

Hawking, Stephen 2010, 'ABC World News with Diane Sawyer: Conversation with Stephen Hawking', ABC, 8 June, Available at https://www.youtube.com/watch?v=MJBwKCHjlXI (Accessed 18 February 2020)

Hemingway, Ernest 1929, A Farewell to Arms, New York, US: Charles Scribner's Sons.

Nhất Hạnh, Thích 1996, Living Buddha, Living Christ, London, UK: Rider, Penguin.

Mother Teresa 2002, reproduced in Edward Le Joly and Jaya Chaliha (eds.), Mother Teresa's Reaching Out in Love – Stories told by Mother Teresa, New York, USA: Barnes & Noble, p. 122.

Einstein, Albert 1930, reproduced in Walter Isaacson (ed.), Einstein: His Life and Universe, 2007, New York, USA: Simon & Schuster, p. 367.

Oliver, Mary 1992, 'The Summer Day', New and Selected Poems, Boston, MA, USA: Beacon Press.

Wittgenstein, Ludwig 1916, Notebooks 1914-1916, printed in 1961, New York, USA: Harper.

Einstein, Albert 1929, 'What Life Means to Einstein: An Interview by George Sylvester Viereck', The Saturday Evening Post, 26 October 1929, p. 17.

Parton, Dolly 2015, 'If you want the rainbow, you gotta put up with the rain' posted on Twitter, 17 February. Available at https://twitter.com/dollyparton/status/567789578342645760?lang=en (Accessed: 18 February 2020)

Glossary

Term	Definition
Adolescence	The period of time in your life after puberty has begun, during which you continue to develop until you become an adult. You are legally considered an adult at the age of 18, but your brain-body continues to mature until around the age of 25.
Adrenaline	A hormone that is secreted by the adrenal glands. Adrenaline increases the rate of blood circulation, in your body as well as your breathing, and carbohydrate metabolism. It prepares your muscles for strenuous activity.
Amygdala	The almond-shaped structure consisting of grey matter, located on each side (hemisphere) of the brain. It is involved with the experiencing of emotions and emotional memory. Otherwise known as Bob.
Anthropology	The scientific study of humans, and their behaviours, societies and cultures.
Bob	The name I give to your two amygdala, and sometimes to your whole 'emotional brain' or limbic system.

Brain

The most complex organ in your body which is the centre of your nervous system. The brain is responsible for your thoughts, your awareness of the environment around you and the starting point for all body movements.

Brain-Body

Your brain-body is the combination of your thoughts, feelings, beliefs, actions and your physical body.

Brain stem

The stem structure at the base of the brain that connects to the spinal cord. All messages between the brain and the rest of the body go through the brain stem. It controls basic body functions like breathing, swallowing, heart rate, blood pressure, consciousness and when to be awake or asleep.

Central Nervous System (CNS)

The combination of the brain and the spinal cord. The CNS controls most functions of the body and mind.

Concept

A concept is an idea or mental image in the mind.

Construct

An idea or theory based on your experiences and beliefs rather than on measurable evidence.

Cortex	The wrinkly, outer layer of the brain full of neurons. It has four different areas (called lobes): frontal, parietal, temporal and occipital.
Co-regulation	The ability to calm your emotions through mental and physical effort along with the support of another person.
Cortisol	A stress hormone made by the adrenal glands that works with the brain to control your mood, motivation and fear. It fuels the body in your fight-flight instinct in a crisis. It also controls the body's metabolism and immune response, and helps with memory formation.
Doctorate	The highest academic degree awarded by a university or other educational organisation.
Emotion	The brain's electrical and chemical response to a stimulus such as a thought, action or situation. Emotions cause feelings, such as happiness, anger, sadness and anxiety.
Emotional Brain	The limbic system and Bob form your emotional brain. It's the part of your brain that acts on instinct rather than logical thought.

Emotional Regulation
>The ability to manage emotional responses without becoming overly distressed or excited.

Epigenetics
>The study of how organisms in the body change and adapt as a result of the way your genes are switched on or off because of your environment or experiences.

Executive Functions
>The mental processes that enable you to plan, focus attention, remember instructions and manage demands of multiple tasks successfully. The brain needs the functions in order to filter distractions, prioritise tasks, set and achieve goals and control impulses.

Explicit Memories
>One of the two forms of long-term memory. The conscious and intentional recollection of facts, information, experiences and concepts.

Firing and Wiring
>'Neurons that fire together, wire together.' Donald Hebb, 1949. When neural pathways in the brain form and are reinforced through repeated experience.

Genes
>A unit of DNA that controls your biological traits, passed down from parent to child.

Hippocampus	Part of the brain's emotion and memory centre.
Hormones	A chemical produced by cells in the body and released into the bloodstream to send a message to another part of the body. It is often referred to as a 'chemical messenger'.
Hypervigilance	An enhanced awareness of your surroundings, feelings and potential threats creating high levels of anxiety.
Hypothalamus	Brain region which works with the amygdala to manage emotional activity.
Implicit Memories	One of the two forms of long-term memory. It cannot be consciously recalled but affects thoughts and behaviours.
Individuate	The process of separating your identity from the identity of another person in order to become aware of yourself as an individual.
Limbic System	A complex set of structures in the brain responsible for emotions such as fear, pleasure and anger, memory, instinct and mood.
Maxim	A general idea considered as truth, underlying principle or rule.

Metacognition   The awareness and understanding of your own thinking patterns and processes. Your thinking about your thinking.

Mind   What enables you to be aware of the world and your experiences. It enables you to think and to feel and create conscious thought.

Myelin   A protein-rich whitish insulating sheath around nerve fibres, which increase the speed of electrical messages through the brain and body.

Neural Network   A complex group of connections within your brain and nervous system.

Neural Pathways   Pathways connecting brain cells and nerve cells to enable a signal to be sent from one region of the brain and nervous system to another.

Neurodiverse/Neuro A-typical
Differences in brain function and social behaviour found within the normal range of the human population.

Neuron   A brain cell or nerve cell that receives and sends electrical signals throughout the body.

Neuroplasticity   The ability of the brain to adapt to its environment and experiences.

Neuroscience   The group of science areas which deal
with the structure or function of the
nervous system and brain.

Neurotransmitter   A chemical which enables the transfer
of electrical signals between brain
structures, nerve fibres and muscle
fibres.

Neurotypical   Brain and behaviour patterns shared by
the majority of human brains.

Oxytocin   A hormone released by the pituitary
gland that causes intense feelings of
bonding, attachment and love.

Parasympathetic Nervous System (PNS)
Part of the autonomic nervous system
known as the rest and digest system. It
conserves energy, slows the heart rate,
increases digestion activity, and relaxes
the body. It's responsible for calming you
back down after anxiety or upset.

Peers   Someone of the same age, social group
and level of authority as yourself.

Philosopher   Someone who challenges commonly held
thoughts, ideas and conventions.

Philosophy   The study of the nature of knowledge,
reality and existence.

Point of Reference — Something that helps you to define or understand a situation, or communicate your understanding to someone else.

Prefrontal Cortex — The area of the brain found at the front of the cortex responsible for highly complex and sophisticated thought including predicting, planning and organising and as well as deciding on social conduct.

Pruning — The physical reduction and removal of neurons and pathways in the brain.

Psychotherapist — A mental health professional who has been trained to treat people experiencing emotional difficulties or problems.

Puberty — The time in life during which your body becomes sexually mature and capable of reproduction. This usually happens between age 10 and 14 for girls, and age 12 and 16 for boys.

REM or Rapid Eye Movement — A stage of deep sleep when your eyes and eye muscles move quickly in different directions while closed. Scientists think that dreams occur during REM sleep.

Reward Pathway — The structures of the brain that are involved in the positive reinforcement of pleasurable activities. The chemical dopamine is activated during any pleasurable activities and can increase the drive to repeat these activities.

Rewiring

The adaptation of the brain's neural pathways through new experiences and learning. Your brain is continuously rewiring itself.

Self

Your sense of what makes you uniquely you and not someone else.

Self-Determination

The process by which you control your own life and decide things for yourself.

Self-Fulfilling Prophecy

A belief or expectation that you hold that proves accurate because of the belief or expectation.

Self-Regulation

Your ability to manage your emotions and feelings without losing control, and to calm yourself down after a difficult experience.

Sensory Processing

The method by which the brain and nervous system receive messages from the senses and turn them into appropriate emotional, mental or physical responses.

Social Anxiety   Debilitating self-conciousness and
                      emotional and/or physical discomfort in
                      social situations.

Socratic Method   A way of using discussion and direct
                      questions to encourage critical thinking
                      and thoroughly examine ideas and
                      assumptions.

Sympathetic Nervous System (SNS)
                      The part of the autonomic nervous
                      system known as fight or flight that
                      reacts to threats, and increases heart rate
                      and blood pressure.

Temperament   A person or animal's nature including
                      their ways of thinking, being and doing.

The CHOOSE YOU! Process
                      A six-step process which consists of
                      identifying particular things you'd like
                      to focus on to help you feel happier.
                      Following the steps allows you to
                      maximise your potential and ability to
                      think and behave in healthy ways towards
                      yourself. The steps are: NAME IT!,
                      CLAIM IT!, REFRAME IT!, TAME IT!,
                      RECLAIM IT! and NO SHAME!

Thinking Brain   The region of your brain formed by the cortex, pre-frontal cortex and other structures to create understanding, and conscious, logical thought.

Tribe   A social group linked by social, religious or familial ties, with a common culture, vocabulary and dialect.

Trusted Adult   Someone over 18 who you trust and feel safe with and has a responsible role in your life or community.

Working Memory   Your capacity for temporarily holding information in mind. Working memory is important for reasoning, decision-making and appropriate behaviour.

World View   How you expect things to work out in your life and in the world around you.

Zone of Proximal Development (ZPD)
    The zone of understanding, learning and potential just beyond your immediate experience or current ability. You access this zone by support from someone who is more competent in that area of learning or from a resource that guides you from where you are now. Your ZPD is always shifting as you develop and learn more.

FURTHER RESOURCES

The CHOOSE YOU! Process

Use these empty grids for any dots you uncover. You can come back to this book at any time to add more dots and work through **The CHOOSE YOU! Process**.

I NAME IT!

E.g. I can be very sensitive and often get upset too easily by things people say.

1	
2	
3	
4	
5	
6	
7	
8	
9	
10	
11	
12	
13	
14	

I CLAIM IT!

E.g. Being sensitive is part of who I am at the moment.

1	
2	
3	
4	
5	
6	
7	
8	
9	
10	
11	
12	
13	
14	

I REFRAME IT!

E.g. Being sensitive means I can notice other people's feelings and be a good friend.

1	
2	
3	
4	
5	
6	
7	
8	
9	
10	
11	
12	
13	
14	

I TAME IT!

E.g. Laughing with Sarah lets me know I'm valued which stops me worrying so much.

1	
2	
3	
4	
5	
6	
7	
8	
9	
10	
11	
12	
13	
14	

I RECLAIM IT!

E.g. I can choose to try to understand what others mean instead of assuming they're criticising me.

1	
2	
3	
4	
5	
6	
7	
8	
9	
10	
11	
12	
13	
14	

NO SHAME!

E.g. I'm sensitive, unique and caring and I'm learning to understand myself

1

2

3

4

5

6

7

8

9

10

11

12

13

14

ACKNOWLEDGEMENTS

The grateful bit!
So many people have helped me bring this book to completion and it is a pleasure to be able to acknowledge them.

I'm especially thankful to and proud of my former pupils and all my patients who have repeatedly shown me the multitude of ways young people can be a true inspiration. I've worked with them in lots of schools, at the Tavistock and Portman NHS Trust and in my private practice. I hope this book will be a suitable way to honour the trust you've placed in me and the determination you've shown throughout your lives. You've been my greatest teachers and my richest source of understanding.

At the Tavi, my tutors and colleagues taught me the value of self-acceptance and self-understanding and how these can transform young people's lives. I owe so much gratitude to Amanda Mintowt-Czyz, Dr Graham Music, Tatiana Nieto, Nina Wessels, Julia Granville, Phillip McGill and Pauline Williams. And to Dr Robert Snell, a heartfelt thank you.

I'm hugely grateful to Nic Farrell and Nia Williams and the whole team at Studio Press who always make sure things flow smoothly, even during a global pandemic! I feel lucky to have the support of Helen Wicks, who has believed in me and my work, and my editor, Frankie Jones, who has provided encouragement and expertise through every stage of pulling this book together. My thanks also go to Brett Dryden for his work to make sure that Chapter Seven was the clearest and most useful it could be.

I'd like to thank my friends and family for their generous and unbegrudging support, often in the form of copious cups of tea and coffee. In particular, Mike Coombes, Sarah Siggs, Helen Baxter, Carol Scholes and Lisa Humphrey – you kept me believing and made everything easier. Simonne Gnessen, your clarity and guidance was liberating.

The sentimental bit!
My grandfather ensured I had the books I needed to feed my mind while my nanna showed me you can do anything you set that mind to, and she inspired lots of the ideas in this book. My parents understood that learning helped me to know and grow myself, and my brave and hardworking mum gave me the idea to write books back before I could even hold a pen in my left hand – thanks, Mum!

Finally, to my own grown children. For everything I've learnt from you and for your patience and love, thank you.